Healthy SLOW COOKER Recipes

Healthy SLOW COOKER Recipes

This edition published by Cottage Door Press, LLC, in 2019.
First published 2015 by Parragon Books, Ltd.

5005 Newport Drive, Rolling Meadows, Illinois 60008

New recipes by Georgina Fuggle
New photography, including cover photography, by Mike Cooper
Home economy for new photography by Lincoln Jefferson
Additional images courtesy of Shutterstock and iStock.

ISBN: 978-1-68052-897-8

Printed in China

Love Food™ is an imprint of Cottage Door Press, LLC.
Parragon Books® and the Parragon® logo are registered trademarks of Cottage Door Press, LLC.

NOTES FOR THE READER

This book uses standard kitchen measuring spoons and cups. All spoon and cup measurements are level unless otherwise indicated. Unless otherwise stated, milk is assumed to be whole, eggs are large, individual vegetables are medium, and pepper is freshly ground black pepper. Unless otherwise stated, all root vegetables should be peeled prior to using. People with nut allergies should be aware that some of the prepared ingredients used in the recipes in this book may contain nuts.

Garnishes, decorations, and serving suggestions are all optional and not necessarily included in the recipe ingredients or method. The times given are only an approximate guide. Preparation times differ according to the techniques used by different people and the cooking times may also vary from those given. Optional ingredients, variations, or serving suggestions have not been included in the time calculations.

Contents

INTRODUCTION

Slow cooking has been a revered cooking technique since ancient times. It is, quite simply, the best way to produce healthy vegetable dishes with deep flavor and meat so tender it falls from the bone. But with our busy modern lives, slow cookers are a welcome convenience for anyone who is out of the house all day and who wants to return to a delicious, ready-to-eat, home-cooked meal.

Since its invention in the 1970s, the slow cooker has gained a reputation as a great cooking gadget for producing finished meals with minimal effort. The slow cooker doesn't provide convenience at the expense of quality or flavor. In fact, it can produce dishes—ranging from starters to desserts—that are full of nutrients and taste fantastic. As meat, stock, vegetables, and herbs simmer together, their flavors emerge, intensify, and marry into a whole that is far more enticing than the ingredients might suggest.

The slow cooker is ideal for making flavor-packed stocks and soups, turning economical cuts of meat into rich stews, and transforming dried beans and root vegetables into wholesome meals. It is also great for cooking more delicate meats, fish, and vegetables, because the ingredients are cooked gently without being broken down. More surprisingly the slow cooker can be used to cook cakes and other desserts—this comes in handy when you don't want to heat up your kitchen during hot weather or if you are using your oven for a turkey or a roast.

Because the slow cooker uses very little electricity (less than a light bulb!), it is both safe and economical to turn it on in the morning and leave it unattended all day. And because the temperature is low and constant, the majority of dishes won't overcook, even after being left for 8 hours or more.

Just think about it for a moment—what could be better than to arrive home after a long day to be greeted by the enticing aroma of a ready-to-eat home-cooked meal?

CHOOSING THE RIGHT SLOW COOKER

There is a vast array of slow cookers—from tiny models to giant pots, each coming with or without a myriad of options and special features. Take time to determine which slow cooker is right for you. They vary widely in price, from the most basic and inexpensive models to high-tech computerized machines. The good news is that it is possible to find a good-quality slow cooker in any price range. Small models with only the most basic settings are surprisingly affordable.

SIZE AND SHAPE

A 4 quart slow cooker is ideal for a family of four or five, while a 2 quart cooker might be perfect for a couple. Larger cookers are great for large families, people who entertain, or those who like to cook a big dish and freeze leftovers. Many recipes here can be prepared in a 4 quart slow cooker, but some slow cookers may need liquid volumes adjusted where ingredients need to be covered.

For most dishes—soups, stews, and the like—the shape of the slow cooker is irrelevant, but some dishes are better suited to a particular shape. Oval slow cookers can easily fit big roasts, turkey breasts, leg shanks, and other large cuts of meat. If you plan to make a lot of cakes, a round slow cooker is a better bet. Models vary from one manufacturer to another, so check the instructions, although the basics will apply to all models.

PROGRAMMABILITY

The most basic slow cooker models offer three settings: high, low, and off. These models are inexpensive and work just fine, but for models with no built-in timer you'll need a separate timer so you can program the correct cooking time.

More expensive models often offer programming features that range from multiple time/temperature settings (such as "high 4 hours" or "low 8 hours") to an automatic switch-to-warm feature. Other models allow you to set your own parameters for temperature and timing down to the minute. The more control you have over the settings, the more flexibility you have—and the more you'll pay for the privilege.

If you plan to use your slow cooker mostly when you will be around the house, a basic model may suit you. If, on the other hand, you hope to set your cooker in the morning before heading off to work for the day, consider one that includes a built-in timer and will automatically switch to "warm" when the time is up.

VERSATILITY

Most slow cookers come with a ceramic cooking vessel that is too porous for use on the cooktop. There are, however, a few high-end models with cooking inserts that can go from cooktop to slow cooker and back again. You'll pay for this luxury, but you'll save time and energy by not having to transfer ingredients from one pot to another and reduce the number of dishes you need to wash. Some slow cookers are portable and come fitted with hinged locking lids, carrying handles, and specially designed carrying cases and straps to help you transport food easily.

A few of the recipes in this book need a metal trivet. This is sometimes useful when you are baking bread or cakes or when roasting a chicken so that the chicken doesn't sit on the base of the slow cooker and become scorched. Some slow cookers come with a trivet. If yours doesn't, then you can use aluminum foil shaped into balls or into a ring to support the ingredient. Other options for slow cooker trivets are a metal canning ring or a large onion cut into big chunks to support the baking container or ingredient.

CLEANING, MAINTENANCE, AND SAFETY

Do follow the manufacturer's guidelines for cleaning and maintaining your slow cooker.

While the glass lid of many models is dishwasher safe, the ceramic pot that comes with most models is not. This is because the ceramic material is porous, which is what makes it retain heat. Submerging it in water for long periods will cause it to absorb water and affect its ability to retain heat. Unless your slow cooker's manual says that it is dishwasher safe, wash it by hand and never leave it submerged in water for a long period. If you encounter stuck-on food, fill it with warm soapy water and leave it to soak for a little while before scrubbing it out.

Be careful never to plunge the hot ceramic pot into cold water as this sudden temperature change may cause it to crack. Instead, fill it with warm water or, better still, allow the pot to cool before cleaning it. The electric base should never be submerged in water. To clean it, unplug it and then use a damp sponge or cloth to wipe off any food that may have dripped onto the outside of the slow cooker.

TIPS FOR SUCCESS

The outer casing and lid may become very hot during cooking, so place the cooker so that it is not too close to walls, curtains, cords, or other flammable items when it is in use. Use oven gloves when touching any part of the slow cooker after it has been on for any period of time.

Always keep refrigerated foods cold until you are ready to add them to the slow cooker. If using frozen meat, poultry, fish, or shellfish, it is best to thaw it thoroughly before adding to the slow cooker. If you choose to add it while it is still frozen, you may need to adjust the final cooking time to ensure that the meat is thoroughly cooked.

The slow cooker allows you to set it and forget it, but many foods benefit from a little preparation. Browning meat, for example, contributes to the overall flavor of a dish and seals in the meat's juices, keeping it from drying out during cooking.

Don't balk at the slow cooking times. The longer and slower your food cooks, the more time it has to develop the depth of flavor that makes it delicious.

Because slow cooker lids are designed to be more or less airtight, sauces and stocks won't reduce the way they do on the cooktop. Because of this, adding too much liquid to your slow cooker can render meat dry, vegetables flavorless, and sauces bland. Since the slow cooker retains all the ingredients' natural moisture, a minimal amount of added liquid is sufficient for most dishes. If, however, you are cooking a dish where you'd like to have a thick sauce, try setting the lid of the slow cooker ajar for the last hour or so of cooking—this allows steam to escape and the liquid to reduce. Avoid doing this too early or you'll lose too much of the heat and there is a danger that your food may not cook properly.

COOK IT SLOW

After a quick guide to the classic ingredients used in slow cooking, the recipes that follow are designed to be easy to use—with short ingredients lists and minimal steps—but they never skimp on flavor. Whether your goal is to offer simple, nutritious weekday meals for your family or to impress your guests with a meal that seems to have taken more effort to prepare than it did, you'll find all the inspiration and recipes you need right here. Happy slow cooking!

CLASSIC INGREDIENTS FOR SLOW COOKING

The ingredients suitable for slow cooking can be wide-ranging—as the following pages show—but there are likely to be some favorites that will feature large in the dishes you choose to cook.

POULTRY

The dark meat portions of poultry—drumsticks, thighs, and wings—suit slow cooking. Chicken breasts are also delicious when they are browned first in a frying pan. If your slow cooker is large enough, you can also cook a whole bird.

PASTA, RICE, AND WHOLE GRAINS

One of the benefits of slow cookers is that most of the ingredients, sometimes all of them, can be added at the beginning, leaving you free to do other things. Whole grains such as pearl barley or bulgar can often be added to the slow cooker early in the process. In other cases, ingredients such as pasta and rice will either need to be added toward the end or prepared separately, to serve with the slow-cooked dish.

SAUTÉED VEGETABLES

Onions and garlic contribute significantly to the flavor of slow-cooked dishes, and sautéing them before adding them to the slow cooker deepens their flavor and the taste of the final dish.

BEANS

Beans are perfect for long, slow cooking. Bean stews and vegetarian chilies—like those made with meat—become thick, rich, and deeply flavored after several hours in the slow cooker. It is important to presoak and cook beans prior to adding them to the slow cooker—see the food safety note below.

ROOT VEGETABLES

Hardy vegetables, such as potatoes, onions, carrots, turnips, winter squashes, and fennel turn deeply flavored and tender after long, slow braising. They won't disintegrate but will be fork-tender and rich with the other flavors, herbs, and spices you include.

MEAT

Fattier cuts of meat, such as chuck, shoulder, shank, and rump, are ideally suited to low-and-slow cooking. Less expensive than leaner cuts, you can also use less of these fattier cuts because slow-cooking extracts a meaty flavor that permeates the whole dish. You can trim off the fat before putting them in the slow cooker to give you a healthier result. Browning meat before adding it to the slow cooker also renders a good deal of the fat, so it is recommended for some cuts of meat. The resulting caramelized crust also contributes to the overall flavor of the dish.

SPICES

Adding spices to the sautéed onions and garlic and allowing them to cook for a moment or two will also help the flavors of the finished dish to marry.

FOOD SAFETY NOTE

Dried beans cooked in the slow cooker have been linked to food poisoning. To be safe, soak dried beans for at least 5 hours prior to cooking, and then drain and rinse them, place them in a saucepan, cover with cold water, bring to a boil over medium–high heat, and cook at a rapid boil for at least 10 minutes. Remove from heat, rinse, and drain one more time, and then place the beans in the slow cooker, cover with at least 1 inch of cold water, and cook on low, covered, for about 8–10 hours, until tender. To prevent the beans becoming tough, do not add salt until after cooking.

Chapter 1

NOURISH

Your slow cooker can provide the food to support growth and development and keep you and your family in the best of health.

KALE, QUINOA, AND CAULIFLOWER SOUP

This healthy soup is packed with nutrients and the quinoa gives it extra substance. Serve with crusty bread for a warming lunch.

SERVES: 4 PREP: 20 MINUTES COOK: 4 HOURS 10 MINUTES

- 2½ tbsp olive oil
- 2 small onions, finely diced
- 4 garlic cloves, sliced
- 1¼ tsp smoked paprika, plus a pinch for garnish
- ⅔ cup quinoa
- 8 cups/64 fl oz hot vegetable stock or chicken stock
- 1 small head cauliflower, about 9 oz, broken into very small florets
- 3 cups curly kale, washed and finely chopped
- zest and juice of 1 lemon
- 3½ oz chorizo, sliced
- salt and pepper (optional)
- 2½ tbsp roughly chopped fresh flat-leaf parsley, to garnish
- 4¾ tbsp natural yogurt, to serve

1. Heat the olive oil in a large frying pan. Add the onion and garlic and cook over medium heat for 3–4 minutes until soft. Sprinkle the smoked paprika on top, and cook for an additional minute.

2. Add the onion and garlic to the slow cooker with the quinoa, stock, and cauliflower. Cover and cook on high for 3 hours.

3. Stir in the kale, re-cover, and cook for an additional hour. Season with salt and pepper, if using, and stir through the lemon zest and juice.

4. While the soup is cooking, heat a small frying pan over medium heat. Add the chorizo and fry until crispy.

5. Ladle the soup into bowls, add the chorizo, garnish with parsley and paprika, and add a tablespoon of yogurt to each bowl.

Per serving: 353 cals | 20.7g fat | 6.1g sat fat | 32g carbs | 5.6g sugar | 6g fiber | 14.5g protein | 3.3g salt

PEPPERS STUFFED WITH FARRO, FETA, AND HERBS

Slow cooking the peppers produces a lovely, tender flesh, which works beautifully with the nutty farro and tangy feta cheese.

SERVES 4 PREP: 20 MINUTES COOK: 3–4 HOURS

- 4 large peppers
- 1 cup farro, cooked
- 2 garlic cloves, crushed
- ½ cup black olives, pitted and halved
- 5 green onions, finely sliced
- ⅔ cup/3½ oz feta cheese, crumbled
- 2½ tbsp chopped fresh basil
- 2½ tbsp chopped fresh parsley
- 2½ tbsp olive oil
- salt and pepper (optional)

1. Slice the tops off the peppers just below the stems, remove the seeds, and slice a very thin layer from the base of each one so they will sit flat in the slow cooker.

2. Put the farro, garlic, olives, green onions, feta, herbs, and oil in a large mixing bowl, and combine well. Season with salt and pepper, if using.

3. Using a large spoon, stuff the mixture into the peppers, add the pepper tops, and then place them in the base of the slow cooker. Cover and cook on high for 3–4 hours, until the peppers are tender. Serve immediately.

Top Tip

USE ROBUST PEPPERS THAT ARE ABLE TO WITHSTAND SLOW COOKING— IF THEY ARE TOO SMALL THEY HAVE A TENDENCY TO COLLAPSE.

Per serving: 295 cals | 15.8g fat | 5.1g sat fat | 30.2g carbs | 8.5g sugar | 6.4g fiber | 8.3g protein | 1g salt

BLACK BEAN CHILI WITH SMOKED CHIPOTLE AND RED PEPPER

This delicious, lightly smoked chili combines black beans and chipotle. Full of goodness, this is ideal comfort food.

SERVES 4 PREP: 25 MINUTES COOK: 8 HOURS

- 1⅓ cups dried black beans, soaked overnight, or for at least 5 hours
- 2⅔ cups/17 fl oz boiling water
- 1 dried chipotle chili
- 2 onions, sliced
- 3 garlic cloves, sliced
- 1¼ tsp ground cumin
- 1¼ tsp smoked paprika
- 1 lb 2 oz tomato passata
- 1¼ tbsp tomato puree
- 3 red peppers, de-seeded and sliced
- 1 large zucchini, sliced
- 1 avocado, sliced, to garnish
- 2½ tbsp chopped fresh cilantro, to garnish
- 4¾ tbsp sour cream, to serve

1. Drain and rinse the beans, place in a saucepan, cover with fresh cold water, and bring to a boil. Boil rapidly for at least 10 minutes, then remove from heat, drain, and rinse again.

2. Pour the boiling water over the chipotle chili and allow it to soak for 5 minutes. Remove the chili from the water, keeping the liquid to one side, and finely slice the chili.

3. Put the chili, onions, garlic, cumin, paprika, beans, tomato passata, tomato puree, peppers and zucchini into the slow cooker. Add the chipotle water, cover the slow cooker, and cook on low for 8 hours.

4. Transfer to warmed plates, garnish each one with avocado and cilantro, and serve with a tablespoon of sour cream on each serving.

Top Tip

THE SMOKY TASTE OF THE CHIPOTLE CHILI IS KEY TO THIS DISH, BUT IF IT IS HARD TO LOCATE, DOUBLE THE AMOUNT OF SMOKED PAPRIKA.

Per serving: 422 cals | 11.6g fat | 2.7g sat fat | 63.3g carbs | 15.6g sugar | 18.4g fiber | 19.6g protein | 0.2g salt

TUSCAN KALE, GOAT CHEESE, AND SUN-DRIED TOMATO FRITTATA

Slow cooker frittatas are light, moist, and flavorful. The goat cheese could be replaced with mozzarella or feta.

SERVES 4 PREP: 15 MINUTES COOK: 3 HOURS 10 MINUTES

1¼ tbsp olive oil, plus extra to brush the slow cooker

1 medium onion, roughly chopped

3 garlic cloves, roughly chopped

3 cups Tuscan kale, shredded

8 eggs, beaten

8 sun-dried tomatoes, drained and roughly chopped

2½ tbsp roughly chopped fresh parsley

⅔ cup/3½ oz goat cheese, crumbled

salt and pepper (optional)

1. Heat the oil in a large frying pan over medium heat. Add the onion and cook over low heat, stirring occasionally, for 3–4 minutes until softened. Add the garlic and Tuscan kale, and leave for an additional 5 minutes.

2. Meanwhile stir the eggs, sun-dried tomatoes, parsley, and half the goat cheese through the onion mixture. Season well with salt and pepper, if using.

3. Lightly brush the inside of your slow cooker with oil, and pour in the frittata mixture. Crumble the remaining goat cheese over the surface.

4. Cover the slow cooker, and cook on low for 2½–3 hours, or until the frittata is set and beginning to brown at the edges. Serve warm, or let cool.

Per serving: 329 cals | 22.9g fat | 9g sat fat | 10.8g carbs | 4.2g sugar | 2.9g fiber | 21.2g protein | 0.7g salt

KOREAN BEEF STEW WITH KIMCHI AND SESAME

Kimchi, a staple of Korean cuisine, marries raw vegetables and spices. Here it adds significant depth of flavor to the stew.

SERVES 4 PREP: 15 MINUTES COOK: 8 HOURS

2 lb chuck steak
3⅓ cups kimchi
1 large onion, sliced
1¼ tbsp grated fresh ginger
4 garlic cloves, crushed
1 bay leaf
¼ tsp pepper
2½ tbsp rice wine
2½ tbsp sesame oil
1¼ tbsp soy sauce
¼ tsp chili powder
⅞ cup/7 fl oz water
salt (optional)
4 green onions, chopped, to garnish
1¼ tbsp sesame seeds, to garnish
4⅔ cups/1 lb 9 oz freshly cooked black rice, to serve

1. Remove any obvious fat from the steak and cut it into ¾–1¼-inch cubes. Place the steak, kimchi, onion, ginger, garlic, bay leaf, pepper, rice wine, oil, soy sauce, and chili powder in the slow cooker. Pour the water over, and mix gently until combined. Season with salt, if using.

2. Cover the slow cooker, and cook on low for 8 hours, stirring every couple of hours, if you can. Remove the bay leaf, transfer to warmed serving bowls, garnish with green onions and sesame seeds, and serve with black rice.

Top Tip

THE STEW WILL BE COOKED AFTER SIX HOURS, BUT THE EXTRA TIME MEANS THAT THE MEAT WILL BECOME ALL THE MORE TENDER.

Per serving: 667 cals | 26.4g fat | 8.8g sat fat | 48.9g carbs | 2.1g sugar | 6.9g fiber | 57g protein | 2.2g salt

BAKED EGGPLANT WITH ZUCCHINI

This Mediterranean-inspired dish combines the familiar vegetable mix of ratatouille in a crumb-topped bake.

SERVES 4 PREP: 20–25 MINUTES COOK: 4 HOURS 10 MINUTES

- 2 large eggplants
- 1¼ tbsp olive oil, for brushing
- 2 large zucchinis, sliced
- 4 tomatoes, sliced
- 1 garlic clove, finely chopped
- 2 tbsp dry bread crumbs
- 1 tbsp/½ oz freshly grated Parmesan cheese
- salt and pepper (optional)
- 16 basil leaves, to garnish

1. Cut the eggplants into fairly thin slices and brush with oil. Heat a large griddle pan or heavy bottom frying pan over high heat, then add the eggplants, and cook in batches for 6–8 minutes, turning once, until soft and brown.

2. Layer the eggplants in the slow cooker with the zucchinis, tomatoes, and garlic, seasoning with salt and pepper, if using, between the layers.

3. Mix the bread crumbs with the cheese, and sprinkle over the vegetables. Cover and cook on low for 4 hours.

4. Transfer to warmed serving bowls, garnish with basil leaves, and serve immediately.

Top Tip

USE EGGPLANTS WITH A SMOOTH, SHINY SKIN—AVOID WRINKLES OR DULL SKIN, WHICH MEANS THE EGGPLANT IS PAST ITS BEST.

Per serving: 169 cals | 5.6g fat | 1.3g sat fat | 27.1g carbs | 15.6g sugar | 10.9g fiber | 6.9g protein | 0.2g salt

WINTER VEGETABLE MEDLEY

Serve this herb-flavored vegetable stew with brown rice or pasta for a tasty and nutritious meal.

SERVES 4 PREP: 15–20 MINUTES COOK: 3¼ HOURS

- 2½ tbsp sunflower oil
- 2 onions, chopped
- 3 carrots, chopped
- 3 parsnips, chopped
- 2 heads of celery, chopped
- 2½ tbsp chopped fresh parsley
- 1¼ tbsp chopped fresh cilantro
- 1¼ cup/10 fl oz vegetable stock
- salt and pepper (optional)

1. Heat the oil in a large, heavy bottom saucepan. Add the onions, and cook over medium heat, stirring occasionally, for 5 minutes until softened. Add the carrots, parsnips, and celery, and cook, stirring occasionally, for an additional 5 minutes. Stir in the herbs, season with salt and pepper, if using, and pour in the stock. Bring to a boil.

2. Transfer the vegetable mixture to the slow cooker, cover, and cook on high for 3 hours until tender. Taste and adjust the seasoning if necessary. Using a slotted spoon, transfer the vegetables to warmed plates, then spoon over a little of the cooking liquid. Serve immediately.

Top Tip

SERVE THE VEGETABLE MEDLEY WITH TOASTED SEEDS OR NUTS ON TOP TO ADD A COMPLEMENTARY CRUNCH.

Per serving: 202 cals | 8.1g fat | 1g sat fat | 31g carbs | 11.6g sugar | 10g fiber | 3.8g protein | 1.3g salt

SLOW-COOKED GOODNESS

A nourishing meal gives sustenance, supports growth, and keeps us in the best of health. It can also make us feel good, give us energy, and stabilize our mood. It's good to know, then, that the staples of slow cooking—from fresh and colorful vegetables to whole grains, meat, and chicken—are bursting with nutrients. So if you are using a slow cooker to prepare your meals, they are likely to have a high nutrient content.

VEGETABLES

Along with fruit, vegetables are the mainstay of a healthy diet. We are advised to make vegetables the majority of what we eat, and a slow cooker makes this task much easier. Root vegetables—such as carrots, rutabagas, turnips, potatoes, and parsnips—are classic choices for slow cooking. Because they are dense, they take longer to cook, in the process absorbing multiple flavors from the other ingredients.

Other vegetables—ranging from spring greens, kale, and celery to artichoke, broccoli, and cauliflower—are also slow cooker favorites. These vegetables are full of fiber, vitamins K, A, and C, iron, and calcium, and being less dense are generally added toward the end of the cooking time. It is also true that naturally sweet vegetables—such as sweet corn, carrots, and sweet potatoes—add a healthy sweetness to slow cooker meals, which can reduce the yearning for less healthy sweet treats.

WHOLE GRAINS

Eating whole grains such as brown rice, pearl barley, bulgar, and quinoa gives you long-lasting energy, and, combined with a balanced diet, they lower the risk of chronic diseases. Whole grains can easily be added to the slow cooker—there just needs to be enough liquid for the grain to absorb. Many slow cooker recipes can also be served with couscous or quinoa, brown rice or wild rice, which are easy to prepare as your slow cooked meal reaches its final stages.

BEANS

From cannellini beans and black beans to kidney beans and black-eyed peas, beans are a rich source of calcium and are also high in fiber and protein and low in fat, sugar, and sodium. It is important to soak beans before cooking, draining, rinsing, and boiling them for about 10 minutes—they will then become deeply flavored after several hours, cooking. Beans are also absorbed slowly so are good for controlling blood sugar or for helping with weight loss.

MEAT

A nutritious meat stew is a classic slow-cooked dish. All meat offers protein, fat, iron, selenium, zinc, and B vitamins. It's the tougher (and cheaper) cuts of meat such as brisket, shoulder of lamb, or chicken thigh pieces that are ideal for slow cooking. This is because the process breaks down the tissue until the meat becomes melting and tender—and packed with flavor.

WHITE BEAN STEW

This rich and healthy stew with white cannellini beans and an array of vegetables has an impressive flavor.

SERVES 4 PREP: 25 MINUTES COOK: 3 HOURS 20 MINUTES – 6 HOURS 20 MINUTES

- 2½ tbsp olive oil
- 1 onion, diced
- 2 garlic cloves, finely chopped
- 2 carrots, diced
- 2 celery sticks, diced
- 1 x 6 oz can tomato puree
- 1¼ tsp salt
- ½ tsp pepper
- ¼–½ tsp crushed dried red pepper flakes
- 1 bay leaf
- 1 cup/8 fl oz dry white wine
- 2 x 15 oz can cannellini beans, rinsed and drained
- 3¾ cups chard, kale, or other winter green, stems and thick center ribs removed, leaves cut into wide ribbons
- 1 cup/8 fl oz water
- 2 tbsp/1 oz freshly grated Parmesan cheese, to serve

1. Heat the oil in a large frying pan over medium–high heat. Add the onion and garlic, and cook, stirring, for about 5 minutes, until soft. Add the carrots and celery, and cook for an additional few minutes. Stir in the tomato puree, salt, pepper, red pepper flakes, and bay leaf, then add the wine.

2. Bring to a boil, and cook, stirring and scraping up any sediment from the base of the pan, for about 5 minutes, until most of the liquid has evaporated. Transfer the mixture to the slow cooker.

3. Stir in the beans, chard, and water. Cover and cook on high for 3 hours or on low for 6 hours. Remove the bay leaf and serve hot, garnished with the cheese.

Per serving: 443 cals | 10.1g fat | 2.2g sat fat | 51.7g carbs | 10.5g sugar | 19.5g fiber | 21.7g protein | 2.2g salt

GINGER-STEAMED HALIBUT WITH TOMATOES AND BEANS

This light and healthy main dish has a fresh and attractive appearance and is full of delicate flavors.

SERVES 4 PREP: 25–30 MINUTES, PLUS MARINATING COOK: 2 HOURS

1¼ tbsp finely chopped fresh ginger

2 garlic cloves, finely chopped

1–2 hot red chilies, de-seeded and diced

2½ tbsp Thai fish sauce

2½ tbsp mirin or other sweet white wine

1¼ tsp sugar

4 halibut fillets (about 1½ lb in total)

1¼ tbsp vegetable oil, for oiling

2⅓ cups green beans, topped and tailed

1 lb cherry tomatoes (15–20), halved, or quartered if large

To Garnish

4 green onions, thinly sliced

finely chopped fresh cilantro

6 fresh basil leaves, shredded

1. Put the ginger, garlic, chilies, fish sauce, mirin, and sugar into a baking dish large enough to hold the fish, and stir to combine. Add the fish, and turn to coat in the mixture. Cover, and place in the refrigerator to marinate for 30 minutes.

2. Meanwhile, brush four large squares of parchment paper with oil.

3. Divide the beans evenly between the prepared squares of paper, piling them in the middle. Scatter the tomatoes evenly over them. Top each pile of vegetables with a fish fillet and some of the marinade. Fold up the packets securely, leaving a little room for the steam to circulate, and place them in the slow cooker. Cover, and cook on high for about 2 hours, until the halibut is flaky and cooked through.

4. To serve, carefully remove the packets from the slow cooker, open them, and slide the contents onto warmed plates, then garnish with green onions, cilantro, and basil.

Per serving: 272 cals | 6.1g fat | 1.1g sat fat | 17.9g carbs | 10.8g sugar | 4.4g fiber | 35.1g protein | 2.3g salt

TOFU WITH SPICY PEANUT SAUCE

Nutritious tofu gets a powerful punch of flavor from a combination of peanut butter, garlic, chilies, and cilantro.

SERVES 4 PREP: 20 MINUTES COOK: 4¼ HOURS

- 2¾ cups/1½ lb extra firm tofu
- 2½ tbsp vegetable oil
- ⅓ cup smooth peanut butter
- 3½ tbsp low-sodium soy sauce
- 3½ tbsp unseasoned rice vinegar
- juice of 1 lime
- 2½ tbsp light brown sugar
- 2½ tsp toasted sesame oil
- 2 garlic cloves, finely chopped
- 1¼ tbsp finely chopped fresh ginger
- 2 jalapeños, de-seeded and finely chopped
- 2¾ cups baby spinach leaves
- 2½ tbsp chopped fresh cilantro, to serve
- 4⅔ cups steamed rice, to serve

1. Slice the tofu into 1-inch thick slabs and pat very dry with paper towels, pressing to release any excess moisture. Cut into 1-inch cubes.

2. Heat the vegetable oil in a large, nonstick frying pan over medium–high heat. Add the tofu, in batches, if necessary, and cook on one side for about 3 minutes, until brown. Turn, and cook on the other side for an additional 3 minutes, until brown.

3. Meanwhile, put the peanut butter, soy sauce, vinegar, lime juice, sugar, sesame oil, garlic, ginger, and chilies into the slow cooker and mix to combine.

4. Add the tofu to the slow cooker. Stir gently to coat, cover, and cook on low for about 4 hours.

5. About 15 minutes before serving, place the spinach in the slow cooker on top of the cooked tofu mixture, cover, and cook for about 15 minutes, until the spinach is wilted. Stir in 1½ tablespoon of the cilantro and serve immediately, garnished with the remaining cilantro, with steamed rice.

Top Tip

TOFU IS A CLASSY SLOW COOKER ACT, THOROUGHLY ABSORBING THE FLAVORS OF THE OTHER INGREDIENTS.

Per serving: 669 cals | 29.3g fat | 4.4g sat fat | 73.8g carbs | 11.4g sugar | 6.6g fiber | 30.5g protein | 1.4g salt

CHICKEN AND APPLE POT

In this recipe, the soft, melting cooking apple adds sharpness while the caramelized eating apples give sweetness and crunch.

SERVES 4 PREP: 25 MINUTES COOK: 7 HOURS 40 MINUTES

- 1¼ tbsp olive oil
- 4 chicken portions, about 6 oz each
- 1 onion, chopped
- 2 celery sticks, roughly chopped
- 1¾ tbsp plain flour
- 1¼ cup/10 fl oz clear apple juice
- ⅔ cup/5 fl oz chicken stock
- 1 cooking apple, peeled, cored, and cut into quarters
- 2 bay leaves
- 1–2½ tsp clear honey
- 1 yellow pepper, de-seeded and cut into chunks
- salt and pepper (optional)

To Garnish

- 1 large or 2 medium apples, cored and sliced
- 1¼ tbsp melted butter
- 2½ tbsp raw sugar
- 1¼ tbsp chopped fresh mint

1. Heat the oil in a heavy bottom frying pan. Add the chicken and cook over medium–high heat, turning frequently, for 10 minutes, until golden brown. Transfer to the slow cooker. Add the onion and celery to the pan and cook over low heat for 5 minutes, until softened. Sprinkle in the flour and cook for 2 minutes, then remove the pan from the heat.

2. Gradually stir in the apple juice and stock, then return the pan to the heat and bring to a boil. Stir in the cooking apple, bay leaves, and honey, and season with salt and pepper, if using. Pour the mixture over the chicken in the slow cooker, cover, and cook on low for 6½ hours, until the chicken is tender and cooked through. Stir in the yellow pepper, re-cover, and cook on high for 45 minutes.

3. Shortly before serving, preheat the broiler. Brush one side of the eating apple slices with half the melted butter, and sprinkle with half the sugar. Broil for 2–3 minutes, until the sugar has caramelized. Turn the slices over with tongs, brush with the remaining butter, and sprinkle with the remaining sugar. Broil for an additional 2 minutes. Remove the bay leaves, transfer the stew to warmed plates, and garnish with the caramelized apple slices and the mint. Serve immediately.

Per serving: 409 cals | 14.9g fat | 4.6g sat fat | 39.1g carbs | 30g sugar | 3.9g fiber | 27.2g protein | 0.6g salt

SOUTHWESTERN SEAFOOD STEW

The flavors of lime and fresh cilantro leaves give this healthy yet hearty fish stew a rich flavor.

SERVES 4 PREP: 25 MINS COOK: 8¼ HOURS

- 3½ tbsp olive oil
- 1 large onion, chopped
- 4 garlic cloves, finely chopped
- 1 yellow pepper, de-seeded and chopped
- 1 red pepper, de-seeded and chopped
- 1 orange pepper, de-seeded and chopped
- 1 lb tomatoes (about 1–2 large), peeled and chopped
- 2 large mild green chilies, such as poblano, chopped
- finely grated rind and juice of 1 lime
- 2½ tbsp chopped fresh cilantro, plus extra leaves to garnish
- 1 bay leaf
- 2 cups/15 fl oz fish, vegetable, or chicken stock
- 1 lb red mullet fillets
- 1 lb raw shrimp
- 8 oz prepared squid
- salt and pepper (optional)

1. Heat 2½ tbsp of the oil in a saucepan. Add the onion and garlic and cook over a low heat, stirring occasionally, for 5 minutes, until softened. Add the peppers, tomatoes, and chilies and cook, stirring frequently, for 5 minutes. Stir in the lime rind and juice, add the chopped cilantro and bay leaf, and pour in the stock. Bring to a boil, stirring occasionally.

2. Transfer the mixture to the slow cooker, cover, and cook on low for 7½ hours. Meanwhile, skin the fish fillets, if necessary, and cut the flesh into chunks. Peel and devein the shrimp. Cut the squid bodies into rings and halve the tentacles or leave them whole.

3. Add the seafood to the stew, season to taste with salt and pepper, if using, re-cover, and cook on high for 30 minutes, or until tender and cooked through. Remove and discard the bay leaf. Transfer to warmed serving bowls and drizzle with the remaining oil. Garnish with cilantro leaves and serve immediately.

Variation

YOU COULD REPLACE THE RED MULLET WITH WHITE FISH SUCH AS COD, HALIBUT, OR SEA BASS.

Per serving: 479 cals | 18.1g fat | 3.5g sat fat | 20g carbs | 10g sugar | 4.5g fiber | 59.4g protein | 1.5g salt

STUFFED APPLES

This simple dessert is much healthier than apple pie but just as delicious—and it is much less labor intensive.

SERVES 4 PREP: 20 MINUTES COOK: 1½–3 HOURS

- 4 large cooking apples
- ¾ cup light brown sugar
- ¼ cup rolled oats
- 1¼ tsp ground cinnamon
- ¼ cup/2 oz butter, cut into small pieces
- 2½ tbsp sultanas
- ¼ cup pecans or walnuts, roughly chopped
- ½ cup/4 fl oz water
- 4 tsp/¾ fl oz heavy whipping cream, whipped, to serve

1. Use a paring knife to cut the stem end out of each apple, then scoop out the core with a melon baller or teaspoon, leaving the base of the apple intact.

2. Put the sugar, oats, cinnamon, and butter into a bowl, and mix together with a fork. Add the sultanas and nuts, and toss to mix well. Stuff the mixture into the apples, dividing it evenly.

3. Pour the water into the slow cooker, then carefully add the apples, standing them up in the base of the slow cooker. Cover, and cook on high for about 1½ hours or on low for 3 hours. Serve the apples hot, topped with whipped cream.

Per serving: 514 cals | 18.9g fat | 9g sat fat | 86.4g carbs | 69.6g sugar | 8.8g fiber | 2.9g protein | 0.2g salt

APPLE, PLUM, AND ALMOND COMPOTE

A stewed fruit compote is a very versatile dish. The almond extract, an essential component, creates a wonderful flavor.

SERVES 6 PREP: 20 MINUTES COOK: 3 HOURS

3 lb cooking apples (9–10 medium), peeled, cored, and roughly chopped

1 lb 5 oz plums (8–9), pitted and quartered

¼ cup brown sugar

1¼ tsp vanilla extract

1¼ tsp almond extract

½ cup sliced almonds, toasted, to decorate

1. Place the apples, plums, sugar, vanilla extract, and almond extract in the slow cooker.

2. Cover the slow cooker, and cook on high for 3 hours. Then stir the contents to break down any remaining chunks of apple.

3. Serve hot, warm, or cold with a sprinkling of sliced almonds.

Per serving: 254 cals | 5.1g fat | 0.3g sat fat | 50.7g carbs | 39.5g sugar | 8.3g fiber | 3.4g protein | trace salt

SLOW AND EASY

Cook the convenient way and leave your ingredients in the slow cooker for a dish with a rich, full flavor.

SPRING CHICKEN STEW WITH CHIVE DUMPLINGS

This warming one-pot meal is incredibly easy to make. The pearl barley and dumplings mean that no other accompaniments are needed.

SERVES 5 PREP: 30 MINUTES COOK: 4 HOURS

1 large onion, finely chopped

3 celery sticks, diced

2 garlic cloves, diced

3 leeks, chopped into thin rounds

8 boneless, skinless chicken thighs

1/3 cup pearl barley

small bunch of fresh thyme

zest and juice of 1 lemon

2 2/3 cups/17 fl oz chicken stock

2/3 cup frozen peas

1 small zucchini, cut into thin crescents

1/2 cup baby spinach

salt and pepper (optional)

Dumplings

1/4 cup/1 3/4 oz butter, softened

1 cup self-rising flour

1/3 cup/1 1/2 oz cheddar cheese, crumbled

1 1/4 tbsp finely chopped fresh chives

3–4 3/4 tbsp cold water

1. Place the onion, celery, garlic, leeks, chicken, pearl barley, thyme, and lemon zest and juice in the slow cooker. Pour in the stock, and season with salt and pepper, if using. Cover and cook on high for 3 hours.

2. Meanwhile, make the dumplings. Rub the butter into the flour and mix in the cheese and chives. Add just enough cold water to bring the mixture together to form a soft dough, and divide the dough into 5–6 small dumplings.

3. Stir the peas, zucchini, and baby spinach into the stew. Add the dumplings to the surface, re-cover, and cook on high for an additional hour. Serve, sprinkled with pepper, if using.

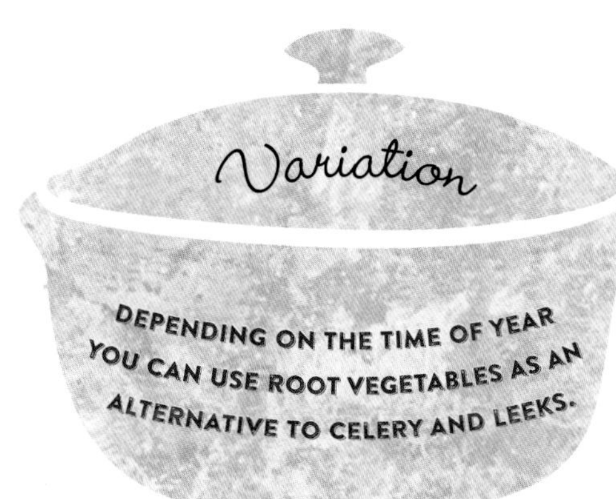

Per serving: 518 cals | 18.8g fat | 8.9g sat fat | 46.1g carbs | 6.3g sugar | 6.7g fiber | 40.5g protein | 2.4g salt

LAMB TAGINE

Slow cookers are ideal for tagines because steam rises up to the slow cooker lid and recondenses before trickling back down into the stew.

SERVES 4 PREP: 20 MINUTES COOK: 7 HOURS

2 lb 2 oz shoulder or leg of lamb, cut into 1-inch cubes

2 onions, roughly chopped

1 large knob of ginger, grated

3 garlic cloves, halved

2½ tsp ground coriander

1¼ tsp ground cumin

1¼ tsp ground allspice

¾ cup medjool dates, pitted and halved

1¼ tbsp clear honey

1 x 14 oz can chopped tomatoes

zest of 1 lemon, keeping some aside to garnish

1 whole cinnamon stick

⅔ cup/5 fl oz hot lamb stock

2½ tbsp chopped fresh cilantro, to garnish

3¾ cup freshly prepared couscous, to serve

1. Place the lamb, onions, ginger, garlic, ground coriander, cumin, allspice, and dates in the slow cooker. Drizzle the honey on top, and add the tomatoes and most of the lemon zest. Add the cinnamon stick and pour in the hot stock.

2. Cover the slow cooker and cook on low for 7 hours, until the lamb is falling apart. Add a little hot water to the tagine, if needed. Transfer to warmed plates, garnish with the remaining lemon zest and cilantro, and serve with the couscous.

Per serving: 772 cals | 30.5g fat | 13g sat fat | 73.9g carbs | 31g sugar | 6.3g fiber | 53.7g protein | 0.6g salt

BOSTON BAKED BEANS

The long slow-cooking process creates a beautifully syrupy sauce in this dish, which is totally irresistible.

SERVES 4 PREP: 20 MINUTES, PLUS OVERNIGHT SOAKING COOK: 8 HOURS 15 MINUTES

- 1¾ cup dried cannellini beans, soaked overnight, or for at least 5 hours
- 1 large onion, cut in half
- 2 bay leaves
- ⅓ cup/3½ fl oz maple syrup
- ⅓ cup brown sugar
- 1¼ tbsp black molasses
- 1¼ tsp chili flakes
- 1¼ tbsp Worcestershire sauce
- 1¼ tbsp dijon mustard
- 7 oz bacon lardons or pork belly, cut into ¾-inch pieces
- ⅔ cups/5 fl oz water

1. Drain and rinse the beans, place in a saucepan, cover with fresh cold water, and bring to a boil. Boil rapidly for at least 10 minutes, then remove the pan from the heat, drain the beans, and rinse them again.

2. Put the beans in the slow cooker with the onion, bay leaves, syrup, sugar, molasses, chili, Worcestershire sauce, and mustard.

3. Stir the lardons into the mixture and add the water.

4. Cover the slow cooker and cook on low for 8 hours, until the beans are tender and the sauce is syrupy. If you can, stir the contents halfway through the cooking process. Remove the bay leaves, transfer to warmed bowls, and serve immediately.

Top Tip

IF YOU LIKE SPICY FOOD, SPRINKLE IN A TOUCH MORE CHILI FLAKES, OR IF YOU LOVE WORCESTERSHIRE SAUCE, INCREASE THE QUANTITY.

Per serving: 687 cals | 14.9g fat | 4.8g sat fat | 110.7g carbs | 39.8g sugar | 16.1g fiber | 31.2g protein | 1.8g salt

SHREDDED BEEF AND PEARL BARLEY STEW

Enriched with porcini mushrooms, this stew has a bold, robust quality. Easy to make, it can also be frozen so is excellent for minimal-effort entertaining.

SERVES 6 PREP: 30 MINUTES, PLUS SOAKING COOK: 7 HOURS 10 MINUTES

- ¾ cup dried porcini mushrooms
- 1½ cups/12 fl oz boiling water
- 2¼ lb rolled beef brisket
- 2½ tbsp vegetable oil
- 2 medium onions, finely chopped
- 3 garlic cloves, sliced
- ½ tsp crushed dried chilies
- 2 tbsp/1 oz butter
- ¾ cup pearl barley
- 3 sprigs of rosemary
- 2⅔ cups/17 fl oz hot beef stock
- salt and pepper (optional)
- 2½ tbsp chopped fresh parsley, to garnish
- mixed salad, optional, to serve

1. Soak the porcini in the boiling water for 30 minutes. Remove the mushrooms, reserving the liquid, and squeeze them dry in your hands. Finely chop the mushrooms and set aside.

2. Season the brisket well with salt and pepper, if using. Heat the oil in a large frying pan, and, using tongs to steady the meat, brown the beef all over for about 6–8 minutes.

3. Place the onion, garlic, chilies, butter, pearl barley, and porcini mushrooms in the slow cooker. Nestle the beef in the center, and add the rosemary sprigs. Pour the porcini water and beef stock around the meat. Cover, and cook on high for 7 hours, or until the beef is really tender.

4. Just before serving, shred the brisket using two forks, and return it to the pot, mixing it in well. Transfer the stew to shallow bowls, garnish with parsley, and serve with a mixed salad, if preferred.

Per serving: 421 cals | 18g fat | 6.4g sat fat | 25.7g carbs | 2.2g sugar | 5.5g fiber | 40.4g protein | 1.2g salt

LOUISIANA ZUCCHINIS

Use a mixture of green and yellow zucchinis for added color in this simple vegetable recipe, which can be served as a side dish for nonvegetarians.

SERVES 6 PREP: 20 MINUTES COOK: 2½ HOURS

- 8 cups zucchinis (about 2¼ lb), thickly sliced
- 1 onion, finely chopped
- 2 garlic cloves, finely chopped
- 2 red peppers, de-seeded and chopped
- 6 tbsp hot vegetable stock
- 4 tomatoes, peeled and chopped
- 1½ tbsp/1 oz butter, diced
- salt and cayenne pepper (optional)
- small baguette or sliced crusty bread, to serve

1. Place the zucchinis, onion, garlic, and red peppers in the slow cooker, and season to taste with salt and cayenne pepper, if using. Pour in the stock and mix well.

2. Sprinkle the chopped tomatoes on top, and dot with the butter. Cover and cook on high for 2½ hours until tender. Serve immediately with crusty bread.

Top Tip

YOU MIGHT NOT THINK OF ZUCCHINIS AS SLOW COOKER VEGETABLES, BUT THEY WORK BECAUSE THE ZUCCHINI SKIN HOLDS THEM TOGETHER.

Per serving: 216 cals | 5.9g fat | 2.7g sat fat | 35.2g carbs | 8.8g sugar | 4.9g fiber | 7.3g protein | 0.9g salt

TAKE IT SLOW

When slow cookers first became popular in the postwar years and then later in the seventies, their main attraction was their convenience. Slow cookers, which were designed to be left cooking all day, helped families achieve a balance between work and home, which of course included having a low-maintenance, nutritious evening meal.

The attraction is the same today. It really is possible to cut, chop, and slice your ingredients, put them in the slow cooker before you go to work, and come back at the end of the day to the tempting aromas and flavors of a healthy meal.

FREE UP YOUR TIME

The novelty of a delicious home-cooked meal where the human involvement is only needed right at the beginning and the end of the process is a liberating experience. Some of the best slow cooker meals that suit the "slow and easy" scenario are soups and stews, because the slow cooker will simmer on a low setting for long periods of time and that way of cooking suits these dishes perfectly. The steam produced during the process, as with a traditional tagine or casserole, will condense on the lid, and then return to the pot, constantly recycling the heat around the ingredients.

PLANNING AHEAD

There is naturally some initial preparation work cutting up vegetables and meat, and it is also true for some dishes that if you fry onions and brown some types of meat before adding them to the slow cooker, then the flavors of the final meal will be fully maximized. However this should not detract from the convenience of the slow cooker, because most of these processes can be carried out the night before. Just put your cooked, chopped, and browned ingredients into the slow cooker dish, and cover and store it in the fridge overnight. Then take the dish out of the fridge and leave it for 20 minutes before turning the cooker on so it has reached the right temperature.

CLEVER TECHNOLOGY

Slow cookers need minimum supervision, and the technology adds to the convenience of the whole process. Once the dish has reached its full cooking time, most slow cookers shift to a "warm" setting, so you arrive home and your evening meal is, quite literally, waiting for you. So all that's required is for you to add a few herbs and to have a plate and a knife and fork ready.

SALMON WITH DILL AND LIME

Slow cooking is so gentle that the delicate flavor of the salmon is retained in this simply cooked fish dish.

SERVES 4 PREP: 20 MINUTES COOK: 4 HOURS

- 3 tbsp/1½ oz butter, melted
- 1 onion, thinly sliced
- 1 lb potatoes (2 medium), thinly sliced
- ⅓ cup/3½ fl oz hot fish stock or water
- 4 pieces skinless salmon fillet, about 5 oz each
- juice of 1 lime
- 2½ tbsp chopped fresh dill
- salt and pepper (optional)
- half a lime, cut into wedges, to serve

1. Brush the base of the slow cooker with 1 tablespoon of the butter. Layer the onion and potatoes in the dish, sprinkling with salt and pepper, if using, between the layers. Add the stock, and drizzle with 1 tablespoon of the butter. Cover, and cook on low for 3 hours.

2. Arrange the salmon over the vegetables in a single layer. Drizzle the lime juice over, sprinkle with dill and salt and pepper, if using, and pour the remaining butter on top. Cover, and cook on low for an additional 1 hour, until the fish flakes easily.

3. Serve the salmon and vegetables on warmed plates with the juices spooned over and lime wedges on the side.

Top Tip

YOU CAN SERVE THIS DISH WITH GREEN BEANS OR PEAS FOR AN ELEGANT LUNCH OR DINNER.

Per serving: 373 cals | 17.2g fat | 6.6g sat fat | 23.7g carbs | 2.3g sugar | 3g fiber | 30.6g protein | 0.6g salt

MANGO BEEF IN LETTUCE CUPS

This tantalizing combination of fresh mango and beef, packed with sweet and spicy flavors, has its roots in Asia.

SERVES 8 PREP: 20 MINUTES COOK: 2 HOURS

1½ lb chuck steak, cut into ½-inch dice

1¼ tbsp cornstarch

1 mango, peeled, pitted, and diced

2 hot red chilies, de-seeded and diced

2½ tbsp soy sauce

2½ tbsp mirin or other sweet white wine

2½ tbsp brown sugar

1¼ tsp sesame oil

2⅔ cups cup-shaped lettuce leaves, to serve

1. Put the beef and the cornstarch into the slow cooker, and toss to coat the beef evenly. Add the mango and chilies and stir to mix. Add the soy sauce, mirin, sugar, and oil and stir to mix well.

2. Cover and cook on high for about 1 hour, then set the lid slightly ajar, and continue to cook on high for an additional 1 hour, until the meat is tender and the sauce has thickened.

3. Transfer the meat to a serving bowl and serve with the lettuce leaves, so that diners can scoop some of the meat into a lettuce cup and wrap it up like a taco.

Top Tip

IF DON'T CARE FOR SPICY FOOD, THEN YOU CAN OMIT THE CHILI PEPPERS—THE DISH WORKS JUST AS WELL WITHOUT THEM.

Per serving: 206 cals | 8.6g fat | 3g sat fat | 13.7g carbs | 10.9g sugar | 1g fiber | 17.4g protein | 0.7g salt

TURKEY AND RICE CASSEROLE

This is a great low-fat recipe if you're counting calories, and the turkey is a refreshing change from chicken.

SERVES 4 PREP: 20 MINUTES COOK: 2 HOURS 5 MINUTES

1¼ tbsp olive oil
1 lb 2 oz turkey breast, diced
1 onion, diced
2 carrots, diced
2 celery sticks, sliced
3²/₃ cups closed-cup mushrooms, sliced
1 cup long-grain rice, preferably basmati
2 cups/15 fl oz hot chicken stock
salt and pepper (optional)

1. Heat the oil in a heavy bottom frying pan, add the turkey, and fry over high heat for 3–4 minutes, until lightly browned.

2. Combine the onion, carrots, celery, mushrooms, and rice in the slow cooker. Arrange the turkey on top, season well with salt and pepper, if using, and pour in the stock. Cover and cook on high for 2 hours.

3. Stir lightly with a fork to mix, adjust the seasoning to taste, and serve immediately.

Per serving: 378 cals | 7.4g fat | 1.3g sat fat | 43.8g carbs | 4.4g sugar | 2.8g fiber | 35g protein | 1.3g salt

STEAK ROULADES WITH SPINACH AND FETA

Rolling steak around a flavorful filling makes for an elegant presentation of a surprisingly simple dish.

SERVES 4 PREP: 20 MINUTES COOK: 3–6 HOURS

- 4 chuck steaks, about 1½ lb in total, pounded to a thickness of ½ inch
- ½ onion, diced
- ¾ cup/4 oz feta cheese, crumbled
- ⅛ cup pitted kalamata olives (about 8), chopped
- 4 small handfuls baby spinach leaves
- ¼ cup/2 fl oz beef stock or water
- salt and pepper (optional)
- a few sprigs of chopped fresh flat leaf parsley, to garnish

1. Season the steaks on both sides with salt and pepper, if using. Top each steak with a quarter each of the onion, cheese, olives, and spinach. Starting with one of the short sides, roll up the steaks into pinwheels, and secure with kitchen string or wooden cocktail sticks.

2. Place the steak rolls in the slow cooker along with the stock, cover, and cook on high for about 3 hours or on low for 6 hours, until the meat is tender and cooked through. Slice the roulades and serve hot, garnished with the parsley.

Per serving: 379 cals | 23.3g fat | 10.4g sat fat | 3.2g carbs | 1.8g sugar | 0.6g fiber | 37.2g protein | 1.3g salt

TRADITIONAL POT ROAST

The ultimate one-pot roast that produces tender meat, perfectly cooked vegetables, and a memorable depth of flavor.

SERVES 4 PREP: 20 MINUTES COOK: 9–10 HOURS

- 1 onion, finely chopped
- 4 carrots, sliced
- 4 baby turnips, sliced
- 4 celery sticks, sliced
- 2 potatoes, sliced
- 1 sweet potato, sliced
- 3–4 lb topside of beef, in one piece
- 1 bouquet garni
- 1¼ cup/10 fl oz hot beef stock
- salt and pepper (optional)

1. Place the onion, carrots, turnips, celery, potatoes, and sweet potato in the slow cooker, and stir to mix well.

2. Rub the beef all over with salt and pepper, if using, then place on top of the bed of vegetables. Add the bouquet garni, and pour in the stock. Cover, and cook on low for 9–10 hours, until the beef is cooked to your liking. Remove the bouquet garni, and serve immediately.

Top Tip

IT'S A SIMPLE TASK TO THICKEN THE COOKING JUICES IN THE POT ROAST WITH CORNSTARCH BEFORE SERVING.

Per serving: 630 cals | 15.2g fat | 5.8g sat fat | 33.9g carbs | 8.9g sugar | 6.5g fiber | 91.7g protein | 1.6g salt

SUMMER VEGETABLE CASSEROLE

This dish uses fresh summer vegetables infused with slow-cooked flavor. You can easily replace the cubed potatoes with new potatoes.

SERVES 4 PREP: 20 MINUTES COOK: 7 HOURS

- 1 lb 2 oz potatoes (2–3 medium), cubed
- 2 zucchinis, cubed
- 2 red peppers, de-seeded and cubed
- 2 red onions, sliced
- 2½ tsp mixed dried herbs
- 1 cup/8 fl oz hot vegetable stock
- salt and pepper (optional)

1. Layer all the vegetables in the slow cooker, sprinkling with the herbs and salt and pepper, if using, between the layers.

2. Pour in the stock. Cover and cook on low for 7 hours. Transfer to warmed serving bowls, sprinkle with black pepper, if using, and serve immediately.

Per serving: 150 cals | 1g fat | 0.3g sat fat | 32.4g carbs | 7.5g sugar | 5.8g fiber | 4.8g protein | 0.6g salt

TURKEY HASH

This is a great-tasting combination as the slightly sweet, nutty flavor of the squash complements the rich turkey.

SERVES 4   PREP: 15 MINUTES   COOK: 7 HOURS 5 MINUTES

- 1¼ tbsp olive oil
- 1 lb 2 oz ground turkey
- 1 large red onion, diced
- 1¼ lb butternut squash, diced
- 2 celery sticks, sliced
- 1 lb 2 oz potatoes (2–3 medium), diced
- 3½ tbsp Worcestershire sauce
- 2 bay leaves
- salt and pepper (optional)

1. Heat the oil in a frying pan, add the turkey, and fry over high heat, stirring, until broken up and lightly browned.

2. Place all the vegetables in the slow cooker, then add the turkey and pan juices. Add the Worcestershire sauce and bay leaves, and season with salt and pepper, if using. Cover and cook on low for 7 hours. Remove the bay leaves, transfer to warmed serving bowls, and serve immediately.

Variation

RED AND GREEN PEPPERS CAN ALSO BE ADDED WITH THE OTHER VEGETABLES.

Per serving: 404 cals | 14.1g fat | 3.2g sat fat | 44.5g carbs | 7.2g sugar | 6.4g fiber | 27.8g protein | 0.6g salt

HAM COOKED IN CIDER

Ham shank makes a great midweek roast and cooking it in this way means that the meat stays moist.

SERVES 6 PREP: 20 MINUTES COOK: 8 HOURS, PLUS STANDING

- 2¼ lb boneless ham shank
- 1 onion, halved
- 4 cloves
- 6 black peppercorns
- 1¼ tsp juniper berries
- 1 celery stick, chopped
- 1 carrot, sliced
- 4 cups/32 fl oz medium cider
- black pepper (optional)

Salad

- 3 medium tomatoes
- 2 small red onions
- 1 cup arugula

1. Place a trivet or rack in the slow cooker, if you like, and stand the ham shank on it. Otherwise, just place the ham shank in the slow cooker. Stud each onion half with two of the cloves, and add to the slow cooker with the peppercorns, juniper berries, celery, and carrot.

2. Pour in the cider, cover, and cook on low for 8 hours, until the meat is tender.

3. Remove the ham shank from the cooker and place on a board. Tent with foil and let stand for 10–15 minutes. Discard the cooking liquid and flavorings.

4. Cut off any rind and fat from the ham shank and carve into slices. Transfer to serving plates and serve immediately with black pepper, if using, and the salad.

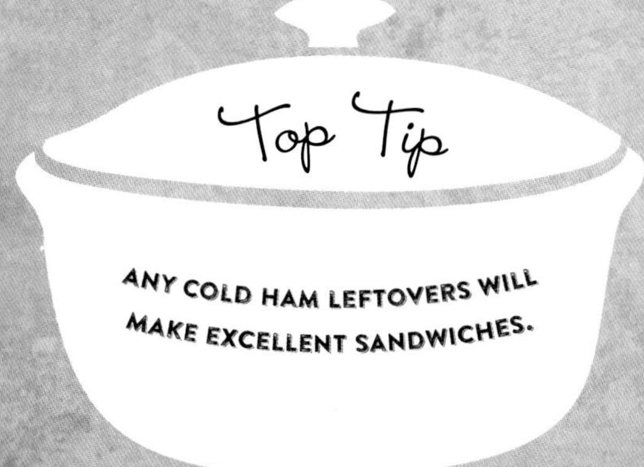

Per serving: 253 cals | 12.7g fat | 4.2g sat fat | 4.7g carbs | 2.7g sugar | 1.3g fiber | 30.4g protein | 3.7g salt

RICE PUDDING

Creamy rice pudding flavored with vanilla is delicious served simply with ground cinnamon. You can also top with a little maple syrup before serving.

SERVES 4 PREP: 15 MINUTES COOK: 2¼ HOURS – 2 HOURS 20 MINUTES

¾ cup short grain rice
4 cups/32 fl oz milk
½ cup superfine sugar
1¼ tsp vanilla extract
1¼ tsp ground cinnamon, for dusting

1. Rinse the rice well under cold running water and drain thoroughly. Pour the milk into a large heavy bottom saucepan, add the sugar, and bring to a boil, stirring constantly. Sprinkle in the rice, stir well, and simmer gently for 10–15 minutes. Transfer the mixture to a heatproof dish, and cover with foil.

2. Stand the dish on a trivet in the slow cooker and pour in enough boiling water to come about one-third of the way up the side of the dish. Cover and cook on high for 2 hours.

3. Remove the dish from the slow cooker and discard the foil. Stir the vanilla extract into the rice, then spoon it into warmed bowls. Lightly dust with cinnamon and serve immediately.

Top Tip

YOU CAN MAKE THE RICE PUDDING IN ADVANCE IN RAMEKINS AND THEN EITHER PUT IT INTO THE OVEN FOR 10 MINUTES OR EAT IT COLD— IT'S JUST AS DELICIOUS!

Per serving: 393 cals | 8.3g fat | 4.7g sat fat | 69g carbs | 41.5g sugar | 1.3g fiber | 10.2g protein | 0.3g salt

SWEET POTATO, APPLE, AND RAISIN COMPOTE

This is an unusual combination for a fruit compote, but the sweet potato is delicious and adds body. Use fresh nutmeg as this improves the taste.

SERVES 6   PREP: 15 MINUTES   COOK: 3 HOURS

1¼ lb sweet potatoes (about 4), peeled and cut into 1¼-inch cubes

1¾ lb apples (about 4), peeled and cut into 1½-inch cubes

⅔ cup raisins

⅞ cup/7 fl oz apple juice

1¼ tbsp clear honey

½ tsp freshly ground nutmeg

¼ tsp ground cloves

½ cup pecans, roughly chopped, to decorate

2 tbsp/1 fl oz heavy whipping cream, whipped, to serve

1. Place the sweet potatoes, apples, raisins, apple juice, honey, nutmeg, and cloves in the slow cooker. Cover and cook on high for 3 hours. Once cooked, stir the ingredients gently to combine them.

2. Put the compote in bowls, decorate with the pecans, and serve with whipped cream.

Variation

IF YOU ARE PREPARING A SEASONAL DESSERT, ADD DRIED CRANBERRIES AND ORANGE ZEST FOR A FESTIVE TWIST.

Per serving: 322 cals | 11.2g fat | 2.3g sat fat | 56.6g carbs | 33.8g sugar | 6.3g fiber | 3.5g protein | 0.1g salt

Chapter 3

COMFORT

Slow cooker dishes have the potential to soothe, console, reassure, and simply make you feel good.

LAMB STEW WITH ARTICHOKE AND ROSEMARY

This comforting stew is given a lift with the inclusion of artichoke hearts, rosemary, and lemon, which work perfectly with the slow-cooked lamb.

SERVES 4 PREP: 20 MINUTES COOK: 5½ HOURS

- 1¼ tbsp olive oil
- 2 lb lamb shoulder, cut into 1¼-inch cubes
- 1 large onion, sliced
- 4 garlic cloves, thinly sliced
- 1¼ cup/10 fl oz red wine
- 2½ tbsp red wine vinegar
- 1¼ tbsp tomato puree
- 1¾ tsp chopped fresh rosemary
- 1 x 14 oz can chopped tomatoes
- 1½ cup artichoke hearts, chargrilled or in brine
- zest and 2½ tbsp lemon juice from 1 lemon
- 1 x 14 oz can cannellini beans, drained
- salt and pepper (optional)
- 2½ tbsp chopped fresh parsley, to garnish

1. Heat the oil in a large frying pan over high heat. Brown the lamb in batches, using tongs to steady the meat, for about 8–10 minutes until the cubes are well colored. Transfer to the slow cooker.

2. Add a little more oil to the pan, if needed, add the onion, and cook over low heat for 3–4 minutes, until softened, adding the garlic for the final minute. Add the wine, and let it reduce by half, for around 5–6 minutes. Add the onion, garlic, and wine to the slow cooker.

3. Add the vinegar, tomato puree, rosemary, and tomatoes to the slow cooker, and mix well. Season with salt and pepper, if using. Re-cover, and cook on high for 4 hours.

4. Add the artichokes, lemon zest and juice, and the beans to the slow cooker. Cover, and cook on high for an hour. Transfer to warmed serving bowls, and garnish with the parsley.

Per serving: 992.7 cals | 52.4g fat | 21.2g sat fat | 64g carbs | 9.7g sugar | 14.3g fiber | 49.7g protein | 1.1g salt

MEXICAN CHICKEN BOWLS

This all-in-one chicken dish is perfect for easy entertaining—the bulk of the work is done by the slow cooker, and the garnish makes it even more inviting.

SERVES 4 PREP: 10 MINUTES COOK: 4–5 HOURS

8 boneless chicken thighs, skin removed, trimmed of fat

6 large shallots, quartered

4 garlic cloves, peeled

1 x 14 oz can black beans

1 x 7 oz can sweet corn, drained

1½ cup brown rice

½ tsp cayenne pepper

1 green pepper, de-seeded and sliced

1 green chili, sliced

juice of 1 lime

1¼ cup/10 fl oz vegetable stock

2/3 cups/5 fl oz boiling water

salt and pepper (optional)

2 small avocados, sliced, to garnish

2½ tbsp roughly chopped fresh cilantro, to garnish

1/3 cup/3½ fl oz sour cream, to serve

1. Place the chicken, shallots, garlic, beans, sweet corn, rice, cayenne pepper, green pepper, and chili in the slow cooker. Squeeze the lime juice on top, and pour in the stock. Season with salt and pepper, if using. Cover, and cook on high for 4–5 hours, until the rice is perfectly soft.

2. Stir through the boiling water to loosen the stew.

3. Transfer to warmed bowls, garnish with avocado and cilantro, and serve with sour cream.

Per serving: 706 cals | 25.5g fat | 7.3g sat fat | 64.9g carbs | 7.1g sugar | 14.2g fiber | 51.9g protein | 1.3g salt

TOMATO AND LENTIL SOUP

Simple yet satisfying and flavored with the warm spices of cumin and coriander, basic lentils can be easily transformed into a healthy bowl of soup.

SERVES 4 PREP: 20 MINUTES COOK: 3¾–4¼ HOURS

- 2½ tbsp sunflower oil
- 1 onion, chopped
- 1 garlic clove, finely chopped
- 2 celery sticks, chopped
- 2 carrots, chopped
- 1¼ tsp ground cumin
- 1¼ tsp ground coriander
- 7/8 cup red or yellow lentils
- 1¼ tbsp tomato puree
- 5 cups/40 fl oz vegetable stock
- 1 x 14 oz can chopped tomatoes
- 1 bay leaf
- salt and pepper (optional)
- 4¾ tbsp crème fraîche
- crusty bread, such as ciabatta, sliced and toasted, to serve

1. Heat the oil in a saucepan. Add the onion and garlic and cook over low heat, stirring occasionally, for 5 minutes, until softened. Stir in the celery and carrots, and cook, stirring occasionally, for an additional 4 minutes. Stir in the ground cumin and coriander, and cook, stirring, for 1 minute, then add the lentils.

2. Mix the tomato puree with a little of the stock in a small bowl and add to the pan with the remaining stock, the tomatoes, and bay leaf. Bring to a boil, then transfer to the slow cooker. Stir well, cover, and cook on low for 3½–4 hours.

3. Remove and discard the bay leaf. Transfer the soup to a food processor or blender and process until smooth. Season to taste with salt and pepper, if using. Ladle into warmed soup bowls, top each with a tablespoon of crème fraîche and a sprinkling of pepper, if using, and serve immediately with toasted crusty bread.

Top Tip

RED LENTILS CAN HAVE DEBRIS IN THEM, SO RINSE THEM WELL UNDER RUNNING WATER.

Per serving: 451 cals | 16.5g fat | 5.7g sat fat | 62.3g carbs | 8g sugar | 8.3g fiber | 17.1g protein | 3.6g salt

SALMON CHOWDER

Salmon and fennel are the perfect match in this recipe, which would make a delicious starter for a special dinner with friends.

SERVES 4 PREP: 25 MINUTES COOK: 3 HOURS 55 MINUTES – 4 HOURS

- 1 tbsp/½ oz butter
- 1¼ tbsp sunflower oil
- 1 onion, finely chopped
- 1 leek, finely chopped
- 1 fennel bulb, finely chopped, feathery tops reserved
- 1 cup potatoes, diced
- 3¼ cups/24 fl oz fish stock
- 1 lb salmon fillet, skinned and cut into cubes
- 1¼ cup/10 fl oz milk
- ⅔ cups/5 fl oz light cream
- 2½ tbsp chopped fresh dill
- salt and pepper (optional)

1. Melt the butter with the oil in a saucepan. Add the onion, leek, and fennel and cook over low heat, stirring occasionally, for 5 minutes. Add the potatoes, and cook, stirring occasionally, for an additional 4 minutes, then pour in the stock, and season to taste with salt and pepper, if using. Bring to a boil, then transfer to the slow cooker. Cover, and cook on low for 3 hours, until the potatoes are tender.

2. Meanwhile, chop the fennel fronds and set aside. Add the salmon to the slow cooker, pour in the milk, and stir gently. Re-cover and cook on low for 30 minutes, until the fish flakes easily.

3. Gently stir in the cream, dill, and the reserved fennel fronds, re-cover, and cook for an additional 10–15 minutes, until heated through. Taste and adjust the seasoning, adding salt and pepper, if using. Serve immediately.

Variation

FOR A FAMILY SUPPER THE SALMON CAN BE REPLACED BY ANY FIRM WHITE FISH.

Per serving: 513 cals | 32.4g fat | 12.4g sat fat | 27.7g carbs | 10g sugar | 4g fiber | 29.5g protein | 2.3g salt

CHICKEN SOUP WITH TAGLIATELLE

Tales that this soup can cure a cold may be far-fetched, but a proper chicken soup is one of the most soul-warming recipes you can make.

SERVES 4 PREP: 25 MINUTES COOK: 5 HOURS 35 MINUTES

1 onion, diced

2 celery sticks, diced

2 carrots, diced

2¼ lb oven-ready chicken

3 cups/24 fl oz hot chicken stock

2 cups dried egg tagliatelle

salt and pepper (optional)

2½ tbsp chopped fresh dill, plus 1¼ tbsp to garnish

1. Place the onion, celery, and carrots in the slow cooker. Season the chicken all over with salt and pepper, if using, and place on top. Pour in the stock. Cover, and cook on low for 5 hours.

2. Leaving the juices in the slow cooker, carefully lift out the chicken and remove the meat from the bones, discarding the bones and skin. Cut the meat into bite-sized pieces.

3. Skim the excess fat from the juices, then return the meat to the slow cooker. Turn the setting to high.

4. Bring a large saucepan of water to a boil, lightly salted if you are using salt. Add the tagliatelle, bring back to a boil, and cook for 8–10 minutes, or until the tagliatelle is tender but still firm to the bite. Drain well.

5. Stir the dill into the slow cooker, cover, and cook on high for an additional 20 minutes. Garnish with extra dill, add a sprinkling of pepper, if using, and serve immediately.

Per serving: 325 cals | 7.5g fat | 2.1g sat fat | 26.2g carbs | 3.7g sugar | 2.5g fiber | 36.9g protein | 1.9g salt

MACARONI & CHEESE WITH TOASTED BREADCRUMBS

This classic comfort food dish is a breeze to make in the slow cooker. A toasted bread crumb topping cooked on the cooktop adds a welcome crunch.

SERVES 8 PREP: 20 MINUTES COOK: 2 HOURS 20 MINUTES – 4 HOURS 20 MINUTES

- 1¼ tbsp vegetable oil, for brushing
- 1½ tbsp/1 oz butter
- 2½ tbsp plain flour
- ⅔ cups/5 fl oz vegetable stock
- 2 cups/16 fl oz evaporated milk
- ¾ tsp mustard powder
- ⅛–¼ tsp cayenne pepper
- 1¼ tsp salt
- 1½ cup/6 oz gruyère cheese, grated
- 1¾ cup/6 oz fontina cheese, grated
- ½ cup/2 oz freshly grated Parmesan cheese
- 3 cups dried elbow macaroni
- 1½ cups/12 fl oz water

Topping

- 2 thick slices (about 7 oz) french bread
- 1½ tbsp/1 oz butter

1. Line the slow cooker with foil and brush with a little oil.

2. Melt the butter in a large frying pan or saucepan over medium–high heat. Whisk in the flour, and cook for 1 minute. Reduce the heat to medium and slowly add the stock, evaporated milk, mustard, cayenne pepper, and salt. Cook, stirring, for about 3–5 minutes, until thick. Add all the cheeses, and whisk until melted. Add the macaroni, and stir to mix well. Transfer to the slow cooker.

3. Add the water and stir to mix. Cover and cook on high for 2 hours or on low for 4 hours, until the macaroni is tender.

4. To make the topping, process the bread in a food processor to make crumbs. Melt the butter in a large frying pan over medium heat until bubbling. Add the bread crumbs, and cook, stirring frequently, for about 5 minutes, until toasted and golden brown.

5. Serve hot, topped with the bread crumbs.

Variation

INTRODUCE EXTRA COLOR AND TEXTURE BY ADDING VEGETABLES LIKE BROCCOLI, CAULIFLOWER, PEAS, OR SWEET CORN WITH THE MACARONI.

Per serving: 593 cals | 29.1g fat | 16.4g sat fat | 54.6g carbs | 9.4g sugar | 2.1g fiber | 28.1g protein | 2.6g salt

CHICKEN AND MUSHROOM STEW

Slow cooking creates tender, rich mushrooms and a superb flavor. This is ideal for a family supper and also a great choice for a dinner with friends.

SERVES 4 PREP: 20 MINUTES COOK: 7 HOURS 35 MINUTES

- 1 tbsp/½ oz unsalted butter
- 2½ tbsp olive oil
- 4 lb skinless chicken portions
- 2 red onions, sliced
- 2 garlic cloves, finely chopped
- 1 x 14 oz can chopped tomatoes
- 2½ tbsp chopped fresh flat-leaf parsley
- 6 fresh basil leaves, torn
- 1¼ tbsp sun-dried tomato puree
- ⅔ cups/5 fl oz red wine
- 3 cups mushrooms, sliced
- salt and pepper (optional)

1. Heat the butter and oil in a heavy bottom frying pan. Add the chicken, in batches if necessary, and cook over medium–high heat, turning frequently, for 10 minutes, until golden brown all over. Using a slotted spoon, transfer the chicken to the slow cooker.

2. Add the onions and garlic to the frying pan, and cook over low heat, stirring occasionally, for 10 minutes, until golden. Add the tomatoes with their can juices, stir in the parsley, basil, tomato puree, and wine, and season with salt and pepper, if using. Bring to a boil, then pour the mixture over the chicken.

3. Cover the slow cooker, and cook on low for 6½ hours. Stir in the mushrooms, re-cover, and cook on high for 30 minutes, until the chicken is tender and the vegetables are cooked through. Taste and adjust the seasoning if necessary, and serve immediately.

Variation

YOU CAN USE DIFFERENT TYPES OF MUSHROOMS—OTHER IDEAS ARE SHIITAKE, CHANTERELLES, CHESTNUT, AND OYSTER MUSHROOMS.

Per serving: 669 cals | 26.1g fat | 7.4g sat fat | 12.9g carbs | 7.6g sugar | 2.1g fiber | 90.2g protein | 1.7g salt

CHUNKY BEEF CHILI

Chunks of beef, onions, garlic, and green pepper are cooked with chili to give just the right amount of kick to this satisfying dish.

SERVES 4 PREP: 25–30 MINUTES, PLUS OVERNIGHT SOAKING COOK: 9¼ HOURS

1⅓ cup dried red kidney beans, soaked overnight, or for at least 5 hours

2½ cups/19¼ fl oz water

2 garlic cloves, chopped

6 tbsp tomato puree

1 small green chili, chopped

2½ tsp ground cumin

2½ tsp ground coriander

1 lb 5 oz chuck steak, diced

1 large onion, chopped

1 large green pepper, de-seeded and sliced

salt and pepper (optional)

4¾ tbsp sour cream, to serve

1. Drain and rinse the beans, place in a saucepan, add enough water to cover, and bring to a boil. Boil rapidly for 10 minutes, then remove from heat, and drain and rinse again. Place the beans in the slow cooker, and add the cold water.

2. Mix the garlic, tomato puree, chili, cumin, and coriander together in a large bowl. Add the steak, onion, and green pepper, and mix to coat evenly.

3. Place the meat and vegetables on top of the beans, cover, and cook on low for 9 hours, until the beans and meat are tender. Stir and season to taste with salt and pepper, if using.

4. Transfer to warmed serving bowls and top with a tablespoon of sour cream. Serve immediately.

Top Tip

SERVE THE CHILI WITH RICE, TORTILLA CHIPS, AND GUACAMOLE FOR A SATISFYING MEAL.

Per serving: 472 cals | 14.6g fat | 6g sat fat | 39g carbs | 7.1g sugar | 12.6g fiber | 484g protein | 0.2g salt

TAGLIATELLE WITH TUNA

When you just want a simple and tasty meal, this is the perfect choice. Serve with some crusty bread, a crisp salad, and maybe a glass of white wine.

SERVES 4 PREP: 20 MINUTES COOK: 2 HOURS 10 MINUTES

- 3½ cups dried egg tagliatelle
- 1 x 14 oz can tuna steak in oil, drained
- 1 bunch green onions, sliced
- 1½ cup frozen peas
- 2½ tsp hot chili sauce
- 2½ cups/19¼ fl oz hot chicken stock
- 1⅛ cups/4 oz cheddar cheese, grated
- salt and pepper (optional)

1. Bring a large saucepan of lightly salted water to a boil. Add the pasta, return to a boil, and cook for 2 minutes, until the pasta ribbons are loose. Drain.

2. Break up the tuna into bite-sized chunks, and place in the slow cooker with the pasta, green onions, and peas. Season to taste with salt and pepper, if using.

3. Add the chili sauce to the stock and pour over the ingredients in the slow cooker. Sprinkle the grated cheese on top. Cover, and cook on low for 2 hours. Serve immediately on warmed plates, topped with black pepper, if using.

Top Tip

THICKER PASTAS SUCH AS TAGLIATELLE CAN LAST A LONGER TIME IN THE SLOW COOKER THAN FINER VARIETIES, WHICH CAN BECOME MUSHY.

Per serving: 486 cals | 19g fat | 7.7g sat fat | 43.3g carbs | 4.6g sugar | 4.2g fiber | 32.8g protein | 2.7g salt

SPICY PULLED PORK

Slow cooking creates pork that's deliciously moist, tender and full of flavor for the ultimate sandwich that everyone will love.

SERVES 4 PREP: 25 MINUTES COOK: 8 HOURS

- 2 onions, sliced
- 3 lb 5 oz boned and rolled pork shoulder
- 2½ tbsp raw sugar
- 2½ tbsp Worcestershire sauce
- 1¼ tbsp yellow mustard
- 2½ tbsp tomato ketchup
- 1¼ tbsp cider vinegar
- salt and pepper (optional)
- 4 hamburger buns, to serve

1. Put the onions in the slow cooker and place the pork on top. Mix the sugar, Worcestershire sauce, mustard, ketchup, and vinegar together, and spread all over the surface of the pork. Season to taste with salt and pepper, if using. Cover, and cook on low for 8 hours.

2. Remove the pork from the slow cooker, and use two forks to pull it apart into shreds.

3. Skim any excess fat from the juices, and stir a little juice into the pork. Serve in hamburger buns, with the remaining juices for spooning over.

Top Tip

ADD A GENEROUS TABLESPOON OF PAPRIKA TO GIVE YOUR MINI HOG ROAST MORE SPICE.

Per serving: 733 cals | 30.1g fat | 10.5g sat fat | 37.9g carbs | 15.6g sugar | 1.8g fiber | 73.5g protein | 3.2g salt

PUMPKIN RISOTTO

This stunning risotto, enriched with nutritious and delicious pumpkin, is a satisfying vegetarian main course for a festive autumn meal.

SERVES 4 PREP: 20 MINUTES COOK: 1 HOUR 55 MINUTES

- 2½ tbsp olive oil
- 1 shallot, finely chopped
- 1 garlic clove, finely chopped
- 1⅓ cups medium-grain rice, such as arborio
- ½ cup/4 fl oz dry white wine
- 5 cups/40 fl oz vegetable stock
- 1 x 15 oz can pumpkin puree
- 1¼ tbsp finely chopped fresh sage
- ½ tsp salt
- ¼ tsp pepper
- pinch of nutmeg
- 1½ tbsp/1 oz butter
- 1¾ cup/6 oz freshly grated Parmesan cheese

1. Heat the oil in a large frying pan over medium–high heat. Add the shallot and garlic, and cook, stirring, for about 5 minutes, until soft. Add the rice and cook, stirring, for 1 minute. Add the wine, and cook for an additional 3 minutes, until the liquid is absorbed. Transfer the mixture to the slow cooker.

2. Stir in the stock, pumpkin puree, sage, salt, pepper, and nutmeg. Cover, and cook on high for about 1½ hours, until the rice is tender. Stir in the butter, re-cover, and cook for an additional 15 minutes. Stir in two-thirds of the cheese, and serve immediately with the remaining cheese sprinkled over.

Per serving: 611 cals | 25.6g fat | 12.7g sat fat | 69.4g carbs | 4.9g sugar | 5.4g fiber | 21.9g protein | 5.2g salt

GO SLOW AND INDULGE YOURSELF

The meals we eat give us energy and valuable nutrients, but the right meal also has the potential to make us feel positive and optimistic. A smooth bowl of tomato soup, for example, will soothe you if you are feeling under the weather, a warming meat stew will warm you up on a cold winter's day—you can even share a plate of divine chocolate cookies with friends on a lazy afternoon as a sublime slow cooker treat!

WARMING FARE

It's not just in the middle of winter that a hearty plate of stew, a chili with some kick, or a smooth vegetarian risotto might appeal. After a long day at work, we look for something to satisfy our hunger and help us relax and de-stress. So if a comforting slow-cooked meal is ready when we get home, then all the better.

TRADITIONAL DISHES

The food we eat has strong associations, and certain dishes can transport us back to a particular time and place, perhaps the familiar taste of a dish that your mother used to make or one associated with sociable family meals. Some comfort meals such as macaroni and cheese or tuna pasta might evoke childhood dinners and remind you of old friends, or a delicious apple crumble served with custard might have formed the much-loved conclusion of dinners with the family.

UPLIFTING MEALS

If you need a meal to lift your spirits and recharge your energy levels, there are also restorative slow cooker options that can put you back on the straight and narrow. Chicken Tortilla Soup, for example, will give you a hearty boost, or Pork Stuffed with Apples combines sweet fruit, salty ham, and crumbly, nutty gorgonzola for a memorable meal you can take your time over. You see, going slow has never had so much to offer!

INDULGENCE

It's hard to resist an indulgent treat, but indulgence doesn't have to be sweet—it can also be full of goodness. This is all about how food makes you feel. Chicken, pork, mashed potatoes, sweet corn, avocado, chili sauce, and melting cheddar cheese are just a few ingredients that, used in the right way with other ingredients that complement them, can cover both indulgent and nutritious bases. The indulgence of a slow cooker meal is often multiplied by the lack of preparation work. A dish might have a long cooking time, but your work could simply be limited to putting the ingredients in the slow cooker and serving with delicious (or indulgent) accompaniments of your choice.

CHICKEN TORTILLA SOUP

This healthy soup is a hearty first course or a light meal in a bowl and will be a surefire favorite in the cold winter months.

SERVES 6 PREP: 20 MINUTES COOK: 4¼–8¼ HOURS

- 1¼ tbsp vegetable oil
- 1 onion, diced
- 1¼ tsp chili powder
- 1¼ tsp salt
- ½ tsp ground cumin
- 2½ tbsp tomato puree
- 3¾ cups/28¾ fl oz chicken stock
- 1 x 14 oz can chopped tomatoes, with juice
- 1 green chili, de-seeded and finely chopped
- 1 lb bone-in, skinless chicken thighs
- 1¾ cup tortilla chips, broken into small pieces

To Serve

- 1 ripe avocado, diced
- 1¼ tbsp chopped fresh cilantro
- 1 lime, cut into wedges
- 5 cups tortilla chips

1. Heat the oil in a large frying pan over medium–high heat. Add the onion and cook, stirring occasionally, for about 5 minutes, until soft. Add the chili powder, salt, cumin, and tomato puree, and cook, stirring, for an additional 1 minute. Add one-third of the stock to the pan, and bring to a boil, stirring and scraping up any brown bits from the base of the pan.

2. Transfer the mixture to the slow cooker. Add the remaining stock, the tomatoes, chili, chicken, and tortilla chips, then cover, and cook on high for about 4 hours or on low for 8 hours, until the chicken is cooked through and very tender.

3. Lift out the chicken using a slotted spoon, remove and discard the bones, and shred the meat. Return the chicken to the slow cooker, cover, and heat on high for about 5 minutes, until heated through. Serve hot, accompanied by diced avocado, chopped cilantro, lime wedges, and tortilla chips.

Per serving: 314 cals | 16.7g fat | 2.8g sat fat | 28.7g carbs | 4.7g sugar | 4.6g fiber | 14.4g protein | 2.7g salt

PORK STUFFED WITH APPLES

This is a great taste combination with sweet apples, salty ham, and pungent gorgonzola to offset the natural richness of the pork.

SERVES 4 PREP: 25 MINUTES COOK: 4–7 HOURS

1 large apple, peeled, cored, and sliced

½ cup/4 fl oz apple juice or water

4 boneless pork chops, about 1 inch thick

4 slices prosciutto

⅓ cup/4 oz gorgonzola cheese

salt and pepper (optional)

2 cups/1 lb 5oz mashed potatoes, to serve

1. Place half of the apple slices in the base of the slow cooker and add the apple juice.

2. Butterfly the pork chops by laying each chop flat on a cutting board, and, pressing down on it with the flat of your hand to keep it in place, cutting through the center horizontally, leaving one side attached like a hinge. Loosely wrap in plastic wrap, and gently pound with a meat mallet to a thickness of about ¾ inch.

3. Open the flattened and butterflied chops like books and place on the cutting board. Layer each chop with a slice of prosciutto, a quarter of the cheese, and a quarter of the remaining apple slices. Fold closed and secure with wooden cocktail skewers.

4. Season the stuffed chops all over with salt and pepper, if using, and place in the slow cooker on top of the apple slices. Cover and cook on high for about 4 hours or on low for about 7 hours, until the meat is cooked through. Serve hot with the mashed potatoes.

Top Tip

THIS DISH IS ALSO A SUCCESS SERVED WITH BAKED POTATOES OR MASHED SWEET POTATOES WITH CRISP GREEN VEGETABLES.

Per serving: 560 cals | 18.9g fat | 9.6g sat fat | 37g carbs | 10.7g sugar | 3g fiber | 57.9g protein | 3g salt

DOUBLE CHOCOLATE COOKIES

Although they look more like brownies than traditional round cookies, these luxurious chocolate treats will win plenty of fans.

MAKES ABOUT 18 PREP: 20 MINUTES, PLUS COOLING COOK: 3 HOURS

- 1 cup plain flour
- 3/4 cup cocoa powder
- 1/2 tsp baking powder
- 1/4 tsp salt
- 1/2 cup/4 oz unsalted butter, softened, plus 2 tsp/1/4 oz unsalted butter for greasing
- 1/2 cup sugar
- 1 large egg
- 1 1/4 tsp vanilla extract
- 2 tbsp plain chocolate chips

1. Generously grease the inside of the slow cooker with butter.

2. Put the flour, cocoa powder, baking powder, and salt into a medium-sized bowl, and mix to combine. Put the butter and sugar into a large bowl, and cream together. Add the egg and vanilla extract, and beat well together. Gradually beat in the flour mixture until well incorporated. Stir in the chocolate chips.

3. Using a rubber spatula, scrape the batter into the prepared slow cooker, and smooth the top. Cover and cook on low for 2½ hours. Set the lid slightly ajar and continue to cook on low for an additional 30 minutes.

4. Leaving the cookie in the ceramic insert, remove it from the slow cooker, and transfer to a wire rack to cool for 30 minutes. Turn the cookie out onto the rack, and let cool for an additional 30 minutes before slicing it into 2-inch pieces. Serve at room temperature.

Per cookie: 121 cals | 7.2g fat | 4.4g sat fat | 14.4g carbs | 6.2g sugar | 2g fiber | 2.2g protein | 0.1g salt

APPLE CRUMBLE

This simple dessert will fill your house with the sweet smell of autumn, and it's the perfect way to end a meal on a chilly evening.

SERVES 6 PREP: 25 MINUTES COOK: 3–5 HOURS

½ cup sugar

1¼ tbsp cornstarch

1¼ tsp ground cinnamon

¼ tsp ground nutmeg

6 large cooking apples, peeled, cored, and chopped

2½ tbsp lemon juice

vanilla ice cream, to serve, optional

Topping

½ cup flour

⅓ cup light brown sugar

3½ tbsp granulated sugar

pinch of salt

3 tbsp/1½ oz unsalted butter, cut into small pieces

¾ cup rolled oats

⅔ cup pecans or walnuts, roughly chopped

1. Put the sugar, cornstarch, cinnamon, and nutmeg into the slow cooker, and stir to combine. Add the apples and lemon juice, and toss to coat well.

2. To make the topping, put the flour, brown sugar, granulated sugar, and salt into a large mixing bowl, and mix to combine. Using two knives, cut the butter into the flour mixture until it resembles coarse crumbs. Add the oats and nuts, and toss until well combined.

3. Sprinkle the topping evenly over the apple mixture, cover, and cook on high for about 2 hours or on low for about 4 hours, until the apples are soft. Set the lid ajar, and cook for an additional 1 hour, or until the topping is crisp. Serve warm, topped with vanilla ice cream, if using.

Top Tip

SPREADING APRICOT JAM ON THE APPLES WILL MAKE YOUR CRUMBLE TASTE MUCH FRUITIER.

Per serving: 474 cals | 16.7g fat | 4.5g sat fat | 82.8g carbs | 59.3g sugar | 5.7g fiber | 4.3g protein | 0.2g salt

Chapter 4

GLOBAL

You can travel all around the world without packing your bags with the help of your slow cooker.

HUNGARIAN PORK GOULASH

This Hungarian staple has the distinctive flavors of sweet paprika, peppers, and tomato. Top the goulash with sour cream for a classic finish.

SERVES 4 PREP: 20 MINUTES COOK: 8 HOURS 10 MINUTES

- 2½ tsp olive oil
- 4½ lb off-the-bone pork shoulder joint, skin off, fat left on
- 2 red onions, finely sliced
- 3 garlic cloves, sliced
- 1¼ tbsp mild smoked paprika, plus a little extra to garnish
- 2½ tsp caraway seeds
- 1 small bunch fresh oregano, leaves picked
- 4 peppers, mixed colors
- 1 x 14 oz can plum tomatoes
- ⅓ cup/3½ fl oz vegetable stock
- 4¾ tbsp red wine vinegar
- salt and pepper (optional)
- 2½ tbsp chopped fresh parsley, to garnish
- ⅓ cup/3½ oz sour cream, to serve
- 1½ cup freshly cooked rice, to serve

1. Heat the oil in a large frying pan over high heat. Using tongs, sear the pork shoulder for 6–8 minutes, until the meat takes on some color and the fat renders down.

2. Add the onions, garlic, paprika, and caraway seeds to the slow cooker, and place the pork shoulder joint on top. Nestle the oregano and peppers around the sides of the pork. Add the tomatoes, stock, and vinegar. Season with salt and pepper, if using. Cover, and cook on high for 8 hours, or until the pork is tender and falling apart.

3. Slice the pork, and deseed and slice the whole peppers.

4. Transfer to warmed plates, garnish with paprika and parsley, and serve with the sour cream and rice.

Per serving: 941 cals | 46.6g fat | 16.8g sat fat | 31.5g carbs | 10.4g sugar | 6.9g fiber | 96.5g protein | 3.5g salt

VIETNAMESE BEEF NOODLE SOUP

You'll find it easier to cut the very thin slices needed for this dish if you place the meat in the freezer for 15 minutes before slicing.

SERVES 4 PREP: 25 MINUTES COOK: 5 HOURS 35 MINUTES – 8 HOURS 35 MINUTES

8 cups/64 fl oz beef stock
1 onion, quartered
2-inch piece of fresh ginger, thickly sliced lengthwise
2 cinnamon sticks
3 whole cloves
2 star anise or 1¼ tsp fennel seeds
2½ tbsp Thai fish sauce
1¼ tsp sugar
2½ cups dried rice noodles
8 oz beef sirloin, very thinly sliced
salt (optional)

Accompaniments, to Serve

1 cup bean sprouts
1 lime, cut into wedges
1¼ tbsp chopped fresh herbs, including basil, cilantro, and/or mint
4 green onions, thinly sliced
2 hot chilies, thinly sliced

1. Put the stock, onion, ginger, cinnamon sticks, cloves, star anise, fish sauce, and sugar into the slow cooker, and stir to combine. Cover, and cook on high for 5 hours or on low for 8 hours. Add salt to taste, if using.

2. Pour the liquid through a fine-meshed sieve or a colander lined with muslin, and discard the solids. Return the clear soup to the slow cooker, and heat on high for about 30 minutes, until very hot, or transfer to a large saucepan and bring to a slow boil over medium–high heat.

3. Just before serving, cook the noodles according to the package instructions.

4. Place a few slices of beef in the base of each of four soup bowls and ladle the soup over to lightly cook the beef. Add some noodles to each bowl. Serve immediately with the accompaniments set out in small bowls for diners to help themselves.

Top Tip

CALLED PHO IN VIETNAM, THIS BROTH IS TRADITIONALLY COOKED FOR HOURS, SOMETIMES DAYS, SO THE SLOW COOKING METHOD IS A PERFECT FIT.

Per serving: 563 cals | 8.1g fat | 3.4g sat fat | 100.6g carbs | 5.6g sugar | 3.3g fiber | 21.1g protein | 7.4g salt

ITALIAN BREAD SOUP WITH GREENS

This healthy, vegetable-packed soup plumps up as it cooks, creating a rich, thick soup that makes the world feel like a better place.

SERVES 4   PREP: 20 MINUTES   COOK: 4 HOURS 35 MINUTES – 8 HOURS 35 MINUTES

- 2½ tbsp olive oil
- 1 onion, diced
- 1 leek, halved lengthwise and thinly sliced
- 8 cups/64 fl oz vegetable stock
- 3 cups kale, chopped
- 2 celery sticks, diced
- 2 carrots, diced
- 1¼ tsp crumbled dried oregano
- 1¾ tsp salt
- ½ tsp pepper
- 7 oz day-old cubed sourdough bread
- ¼ cup/1 oz freshly grated Parmesan cheese, to garnish

1. Heat the oil in a large frying pan over medium–high heat. Add the onion and leek, and sauté for about 5 minutes, until soft.

2. Transfer the mixture to the slow cooker, and add the stock, kale, celery, carrots, oregano, salt, and pepper. Cover, and cook on high for about 4 hours or on low for 8 hours.

3. Add the bread to the soup, cover, and cook on high, stirring occasionally, for about 30 minutes, until the bread breaks down and thickens the soup.

4. Serve hot, garnished with the cheese.

Variation

TURN THE SOUP INTO A ONE-DISH MEAL BY ADDING A CAN OF CANNELLINI BEANS ALONG WITH THE VEGETABLES.

Per serving: 317 cals | 13.6g fat | 4.4g sat fat | 42.8g carbs | 8.4g sugar | 5.2g fiber | 11.8g protein | 8.1g salt

EASY CHINESE CHICKEN

This great-tasting recipe can be served simply with steamed rice or as part of a meal with the addition of a quickly cooked stir-fried vegetable selection.

SERVES 2 PREP: 20 MINUTES COOK: 4 HOURS 5 MINUTES

- 2½ tsp grated fresh ginger
- 4 garlic cloves, finely chopped
- 2 star anise
- ⅔ cups/5 fl oz Chinese rice wine or medium dry sherry
- 2½ tbsp dark soy sauce
- 1¼ tsp sesame oil
- 6 tbsp water
- 4 skinless chicken thighs or drumsticks
- 2 shredded green onions, to garnish
- 4⅔ cups cooked rice, to serve

1. Mix together the ginger, garlic, star anise, rice wine, soy sauce, sesame oil, and water in a bowl. Place the chicken in a saucepan, add the spice mixture, and bring to a boil.

2. Transfer to the slow cooker, cover, and cook on low for 4 hours, or until the chicken is tender and cooked through.

3. Remove and discard the star anise. Transfer the chicken to warmed serving plates, garnish with the shredded green onions, and serve immediately with the rice.

Top Tip

THIS IS A STRAIGHTFORWARD RECIPE TO PREPARE FOR A WEEKDAY SUPPER.

Per serving: 731 cals | 7.9g fat | 1.8g sat fat | 107g carbs | 0.9g sugar | 2.1g fiber | 33.1g protein | 2.4g salt

SAUSAGE AND BEAN CASSOULET

Here is slow cooking at its best, a variation on the famous regional French casserole, named after the pot it's traditionally cooked in.

SERVES 4 PREP: 20 MINUTES COOK: 6 HOURS 10 MINUTES

2½ tbsp sunflower oil

2 onions, chopped

2 garlic cloves, finely chopped

4 oz streaky bacon, chopped

1 lb 2 oz pork sausages

1 x 14 oz can navy beans, red kidney beans, or black-eyed peas, drained and rinsed

2½ tbsp chopped fresh parsley

⅔ cups/5 fl oz hot beef stock

To Serve

4 slices (about 14 oz) french bread

¼ cup/2 oz gruyère cheese, grated

1. Heat the oil in a heavy bottom frying pan. Add the onions and cook over low heat, stirring occasionally, for 5 minutes, until softened. Add the garlic, bacon, and sausages, and cook, stirring and turning the sausages occasionally, for an additional 5 minutes.

2. Using a slotted spoon, transfer the mixture from the frying pan to the slow cooker. Add the beans, parsley, and stock, then cover, and cook on low for 6 hours.

3. Shortly before serving, preheat the broiler. Carefully place the bread slices on the oven rack, and lightly toast on one side under the broiler. Turn the slices over, sprinkle with the grated cheese, and place under the broiler until just melted.

4. Serve the cassoulet with the bread slices immediately.

Per serving: 919 cals | 52.2g fat | 16g sat fat | 67g carbs | 8.5g sugar | 8g fiber | 44.3g protein | 5.1g salt

ASPARAGUS AND SPINACH RISOTTO

Cooking risotto in this way removes the tedious stirring that is usually associated with this classic Italian dish.

SERVES 4 PREP: 20 MINUTES COOK: 2 HOURS 35 MINUTES

- 2½ tbsp olive oil
- 4 shallots, finely chopped
- 1⅓ cup arborio rice
- 1 garlic clove, crushed
- ⅓ cup/3½ fl oz dry white wine
- 3¾ cups/28¾ fl oz vegetable stock
- 1¾ cup asparagus spears
- 1 cup baby spinach leaves
- ⅓ cup/1½ oz freshly grated Parmesan cheese
- salt and pepper (optional)

1. Heat the oil in a frying pan, add the shallots, and fry over medium heat, stirring, for 2–3 minutes. Add the rice and garlic, and cook for an additional 2 minutes, stirring. Add the wine, and allow it to boil for 30 seconds.

2. Transfer the rice mixture to the slow cooker, add the stock, and season to taste with salt and pepper, if using. Cover and cook on high for 2 hours, or until most of the liquid is absorbed.

3. Cut the asparagus into 1½-inch lengths. Stir into the rice, then spread the spinach over the top. Replace the lid, and cook on high for an additional 30 minutes, until the asparagus is just tender and the spinach is wilted.

4. Stir in the spinach with the cheese, then adjust the seasoning to taste, and serve immediately in warmed bowls.

Top Tip

ARBORIO RICE IS USED HERE BECAUSE IT GIVES THE RISOTTO A DISTINCTIVE AND APPEALING CREAMINESS.

Per serving: 422 cals | 11.3g fat | 3.6g sat fat | 65.7g carbs | 2.7g sugar | 4.4g fiber | 11.5g protein | 2.6g salt

BEEF AND CHIPOTLE BURRITOS

Chipotle peppers are smoked, dried jalapeños, used in Mexican cooking for centuries—they add the heat to this spicy beef filling for tortillas.

SERVES 4 PREP: 25 MINUTES, PLUS SOAKING COOK: 4 HOURS 10 MINUTES

1¼ tbsp olive oil

1 onion, sliced

1 lb 5 oz chuck steak

1 dried chipotle pepper, soaked in boiling water for 20 minutes

1 garlic clove, crushed

1¼ tsp ground cumin

1 x 14 oz can chopped tomatoes

8 large tortillas

salt and pepper (optional)

4¾ tbsp sour cream, to serve

2 cups green salad, to serve

1. Heat the oil in a pan, and fry the onion for 3–4 minutes until golden. Tip into the slow cooker and arrange the beef on top. Drain and chop the chipotle. Sprinkle the chipotle pepper, garlic, cumin, tomatoes, and salt and pepper, if using, over the meat.

2. Cover, and cook on low for 4 hours, until the meat is tender.

3. Warm the tortillas. Remove the beef and shred with a fork. Divide between the tortillas, and spoon the tomato sauce on top. Wrap, and serve with the sour cream and green salad.

Variation

SERVE ON TOP OF TORTILLA CHIPS AND TOP WITH CHIHUAHUA CHEESE TO MAKE A RICH TAKE ON NACHOS.

Per serving: 678 cals | 23.1g fat | 8.7g sat fat | 70.6g carbs | 8.4g sugar | 3.5g fiber | 44.1g protein | 1.4g salt

INTERNATIONAL GO SLOW

In our multicultural society, our most favorite meals are not necessarily those with their roots close to home. Many national classics have traveled all over the world and have become an essential part of different food cultures. The Italian risotto, the Spanish paella, the French bouillabaisse, and the Hungarian pork goulash, for example, are all recognized and enjoyed internationally.

These dishes and many more can be created in a slow cooker with all their original flavors and a minimum of fuss. The recipes in this chapter show us how a slow cooker can create the meals that we already love and maybe introduce a few new ones, allowing us to travel gastronomically from Europe to China and from North Africa to New England.

GLOBAL RECIPES IN A SLOW COOKER

It's not a challenge to find slow cooker recipes with global impact. From goulash to tagines and pulled pork to cassoulet, every cuisine has a slow cooking genre. Recipes based on stews or soups probably have the longest food history of all and transfer easily to a slow cooker, where the long, slow cooking process mirrors the simmering of a soup on the cooktop or a stew gently cooking in an oven. Hungary and Spain are just a couple of the countries with national recipes that translate beautifully to the slow cooker. The bouillabaisse, for example, is simplified from the French classic but still results in a delicious stew characterized by saffron, oregano, tomatoes, and succulent seafood.

Slow cooking also suits the Spanish-style Vegetarian Paella, which is cooked in the slow cooker until the rice is tender and the stock absorbed, in the same way as you would cook the paella in a pan over low heat. The ingredients for Italian Bread Pudding would normally be combined in a mold, surrounded by boiling water and baked in the oven. The process is the same in the slow cooker, but the panettone, milk, cream, sugar, and lemon now have two and a half hours to meld with the marsala into a delicious end-of-meal offering.

FROM EUROPE TO ASIA

With your slow cooker, you can enjoy the flavors of Africa, America, Europe, and Asia—where the slow cooking process tenderizes the meat or chicken and infuses the flavors of garlic, ginger, soy sauce, as well as chili (Korea) and fish sauce (Thailand and Vietnam) perfectly.

So, you see, you really can eat your fill, exploring the world from your dining room table, with your trusty slow cooker doing all the work.

NEW ENGLAND CLAM CHOWDER

Many recipes for this fish soup exist up and down the east coast of the United States—some are creamy while others use tomatoes for color and flavor.

SERVES 4 PREP: 20 MINUTES COOK: 4 HOURS 5 MINUTES

- 1½ tbsp/1 oz butter
- 1 onion, finely chopped
- 2 potatoes, cut into cubes
- 1 large carrot, diced
- 1⅔ cups/14 fl oz fish stock or water
- 1 x 10 oz can clams, drained
- 1¼ cup/9 fl oz heavy whipping cream
- salt and pepper (optional)
- chopped fresh parsley, to garnish
- fresh crusty bread (about 6 oz), to serve

1. Melt the butter in a frying pan, add the onion, and fry over medium heat for 4–5 minutes, stirring, until golden.

2. Transfer the onion to the slow cooker with the potatoes, carrot, stock, and salt and pepper, if using. Cover and cook on high for 3 hours.

3. Add the clams and the cream to the slow cooker, and stir to mix evenly. Cover, and cook for an additional hour.

4. Adjust the seasoning to taste. Transfer to warmed serving bowls, sprinkle with parsley, and serve immediately with crusty bread.

Variation

WHEN SERVING THE CHOWDER, YOU CAN ALSO ADD PIECES OF FRIED BACON TO THE TOP OF EACH DISH.

Per serving: 668 cals | 41g fat | 24.6g sat fat | 50g carbs | 4.6g sugar | 4.6g fiber | 24.7g protein | 2.1g salt

MOROCCAN SPICED BEEF STEW

Heady spices and sweet dried apricots come together for an exotic twist on beef stew.

SERVES 6 PREP: 20 MINUTES COOK: 6 HOURS 10 MINUTES – 9 HOURS 10 MINUTES

- 2½ tbsp vegetable oil
- 1 onion, diced
- 1¾ tsp salt
- ½ tsp pepper
- 2½ tsp ground cumin
- ½ tsp ground cinnamon
- ½ tsp ground ginger
- 1 cup/8 fl oz red wine
- 1½ lb chuck steak, cut into 2-inch pieces
- ⅔ cup dried apricots, diced
- 2½ tbsp honey
- ½ cup/4 fl oz water
- chopped fresh cilantro, to garnish
- 5¼ cups cooked couscous, to serve

1. Heat the oil in a large frying pan. Add the onion, and cook, stirring, for about 5 minutes, until soft. Add the salt, pepper, cumin, cinnamon, and ginger, and cook, stirring, for an additional 1 minute.

2. Add the wine, bring to a boil, and cook for 1 minute, scraping up any sediment from the base of the pan. Transfer the mixture to the slow cooker.

3. Add the beef, apricots, honey, and water, and stir to mix. Cover, and cook on high for 6 hours or on low for 9 hours, until the meat is very tender.

4. Serve hot with couscous, garnished with cilantro.

Variation

TO INCREASE THE VEGETABLE CONTENT, ADD A SMALL SQUASH, CUT INTO MEDIUM CHUNKS, TO THE SLOW COOKER WITH THE BEEF.

Per serving: 499 cals | 13.1g fat | 3.9g sat fat | 57.6g carbs | 18.5g sugar | 4.3g fiber | 30.7g protein | 1.7g salt

VEGETARIAN PAELLA

A delicious vegetarian version of the Spanish classic. If you include fish and seafood in your diet, you could add cooked shrimp just before serving.

SERVES 6 PREP: 25 MINUTES COOK: 2¾–3¼ HOURS

4¾ tbsp olive oil
1 onion, sliced
2 garlic cloves, finely chopped
4 cups/32 fl oz hot vegetable stock
large pinch of saffron threads, lightly crushed
1 yellow pepper, de-seeded and sliced
1 red pepper, de-seeded and sliced
1 large eggplant, diced
1¼ cups paella or risotto rice
1 lb tomatoes (about 1–2 large), peeled and chopped
½ cup chestnut mushrooms, sliced
¾ cup green beans, halved
1 x 14 oz can cranberry beans, drained and rinsed
salt and pepper (optional)

1. Heat the oil in a large frying pan. Add the onion and garlic, and cook over low heat, stirring occasionally, for 5 minutes, until softened. Put 3 tablespoons of the hot stock into a small bowl, and stir in the saffron, then set aside to infuse.

2. Add the peppers and eggplant to the pan, and cook, stirring occasionally, for 5 minutes. Add the rice and cook, stirring constantly, for 1 minute, until the grains are coated with oil and glistening. Pour in the remaining stock, and add the tomatoes, mushrooms, green beans, and cranberry beans. Stir in the saffron mixture, and season to taste with salt and pepper, if using.

3. Transfer the mixture to the slow cooker, cover, and cook on low for 2½–3 hours, until the rice is tender and the stock has been absorbed. Transfer to warmed serving plates and serve immediately.

Top Tip

A SOFT-GRAINED RICE, SUCH AS BOMBA, IS USED IN SPAIN—THIS ABSORBS THE STOCK WITHOUT BECOMING CREAMY OR STICKY.

Per serving: 330 cals | 11g fat | 2g sat fat | 50.5g carbs | 9.2g sugar | 9.5g fiber | 8.4g protein | 1.6g salt

THAI BEEF CURRY

Enriched with coconut milk and peanut butter, this simple curry will transport you to Southeast Asia.

SERVES 4 PREP: 20 MINUTES COOK: 5–9 HOURS

- 4 tbsp Thai red curry paste
- 3/4 cup/6 fl oz unsweetened coconut milk
- 1/4 cup dark brown sugar
- 1 1/4 tbsp Thai fish sauce
- 2/3 cup smooth peanut butter
- 2 lb chuck steak, cut into 1-inch dice
- 2 potatoes, diced
- 1/2 cup/4 fl oz beef stock or water
- fresh basil leaves, cut into ribbons, to garnish
- 4 2/3 cups steamed rice, to serve

1. Put the curry paste, coconut milk, sugar, fish sauce, and peanut butter into the slow cooker, and stir to combine. Add the beef, potatoes, and stock, and stir to coat in the mixture.

2. Cover, and cook on high for about 4 hours or on low for 8 hours, then set the lid slightly ajar, and cook for an additional 1 hour, or until the beef is very tender and the sauce has thickened slightly. Serve hot, garnished with basil, with the steamed rice.

Top Tip

THE CREAMY COCONUT MILK TONES DOWN THE HEAT OF THE CURRY.

Per serving: 941 cals | 38.8g fat | 17.4g sat fat | 87.3g carbs | 17.1g sugar | 4.2g fiber | 60.1g protein | 2.2g salt

EASY BOUILLABAISSE WITH GARLIC MAYONNAISE

This simplified version of the French classic is sure to impress. Feel free to add or substitute other types of fish or shellfish.

SERVES 4 PREP: 30 MINUTES COOK: 2½-4½ HOURS

Bouillabaisse

pinch of saffron threads

1¼ tbsp hot water

2½ tbsp olive oil

1 onion, diced

3 garlic cloves, finely chopped

2 celery sticks, finely chopped

2½ tsp crumbled, dried oregano

1¼ tsp salt

¼–½ tsp crushed dried red pepper flakes

1½ cups/12 fl oz dry white wine

14 oz tomato passata

1 x 14 oz can chopped tomatoes, with juice

12 small clams, scrubbed

12 mussels, scrubbed and debearded

1 lb white fish fillet, such as halibut, cut into 2-inch pieces

8 oz raw shrimp, peeled and deveined

2½ tbsp finely chopped fresh parsley, to garnish

Garlic Mayonnaise

2 garlic cloves, finely chopped

½ tsp salt

½ cup/4 fl oz mayonnaise

1. Place the saffron in a small bowl, and cover with the hot water. Heat the oil in a large frying pan over medium–high heat. Add the onion and garlic, and cook, stirring, for about 5 minutes, until soft. Add the celery, oregano, salt, and red pepper flakes, then add the wine. Bring to a boil, and cook, stirring, for about 8 minutes, until the liquid is reduced by half. Transfer the mixture to the slow cooker.

2. Stir in the saffron and its soaking water, tomato passata, and tomatoes with their can juices. Cover and cook on high for about 2 hours or on low for about 4 hours.

3. Discard any clams or mussels with broken shells and any that refuse to close when tapped. Add the fish, shrimp, clams, and mussels to the slow cooker, cover, and cook on high for an additional 10–15 minutes, until the fish and shrimp are cooked through and the clams and mussels have opened, discarding any that still remain closed.

4. To make the garlic mayonnaise, mash the garlic and salt together with a fork to make a paste. Stir in the mayonnaise. To serve, ladle some broth into four serving bowls, then add some of the fish and shellfish. Top each serving with a dollop of the garlic mayonnaise, garnish with parsley, and serve immediately.

Per serving: 649 cals | 34.4g fat | 5.2g sat fat | 20.2g carbs | 10.8g sugar | 2.5g fiber | 47.6g protein | 4.3g salt

KOREAN BRAISED BEEF RIBS

You'll end up with meltingly tender meat in this classic recipe. Ask your butcher to cut the ribs into 3-inch lengths for easy serving.

SERVES 6 PREP: 20 MINUTES, PLUS MARINATING COOK: 6–9 HOURS

- 1 onion, diced
- 3 garlic cloves, finely chopped
- 1¼ tbsp finely chopped fresh ginger
- 2½ tbsp soy sauce
- 2½ tbsp soft dark brown sugar
- 2½ tbsp mirin or other sweet white wine
- 1¼ tbsp sesame oil
- 1¼ tsp chili paste
- 2¾ lb bone-in beef short ribs
- 2 small potatoes, cubed
- 2 carrots, cubed
- 3 green onions, thinly sliced, to garnish
- 1¼ tbsp toasted sesame seeds, to garnish
- 4⅔ cups steamed rice, to serve

1. Put the onion, garlic, ginger, soy sauce, sugar, mirin, oil, and chili paste into a bowl large enough to hold the meat, and stir to combine. Add the ribs, and turn to coat in the mixture. Cover and place in the refrigerator to marinate for at least 2 hours or overnight.

2. Place the beef, together with the marinade, in the slow cooker. Add the potatoes and carrots, and stir to mix. Cover, and cook on high for about 6 hours or on low for about 9 hours, until the meat is tender and falling off the bone.

3. Serve hot, garnished with the green onions and sesame seeds with steamed rice.

Per serving: 521 cals | 19.5g fat | 7.3g sat fat | 51.5g carbs | 9g sugar | 2.5g fiber | 31.6g protein | 1.2g salt

ITALIAN BREAD PUDDING

A great variation on traditional bread and butter pudding—panettone is an Italian fruit loaf available mainly at Christmas.

SERVES 6 PREP: 20 MINUTES, PLUS COOLING AND CHILLING COOK: 2 HOURS 35 MINUTES

- 2 tsp unsalted butter, for greasing
- 6 slices panettone
- 3½ tbsp marsala
- 1¼ cup/10 fl oz milk
- 1¼ cup/10 fl oz light cream
- ½ cup superfine sugar
- grated rind of ½ lemon
- pinch ground cinnamon
- 3 large eggs, lightly beaten

1. Grease a 1-liter pudding basin or 1-quart heat-proof bowl with butter. Place the panettone on a deep plate and sprinkle with the marsala.

2. Pour the milk and cream into a saucepan, and add the sugar, lemon rind, and cinnamon. Gradually bring to a boil over low heat, stirring until the sugar has dissolved. Remove the pan from the heat and let cool slightly, then pour the mixture onto the eggs, beating constantly.

3. Place the panettone in the prepared basin, pour in the egg mixture, and cover with foil. Stand the basin on a trivet in the slow cooker and pour in enough boiling water to come about one-third of the way up the side of the basin. Cover and cook on high for 2½ hours, until set.

4. Carefully remove the basin from the slow cooker and discard the foil. Let cool, then chill in the refrigerator until required. Run a knife around the inside of the basin, then turn out the bread pudding onto a serving dish. Serve immediately.

Variation

YOU CAN REPLACE THE PANETTONE WITH ANY SWEET FRUIT BREAD OR BRIOCHE IF YOU PREFER.

Per serving: 438 cals | 22.5g fat | 11.1g sat fat | 49.2g carbs | 34.2g sugar | 2.6g fiber | 9.6g protein | 0.3g salt

WOW FACTOR

These striking, impressive, and memorable slow cooker dishes are certain to keep your guests talking.

RED THAI CURRY WITH SALMON AND LIME

This flavorful Thai curry couldn't be easier because the slow cooker does all the work. Serve with black rice for a sophisticated, elegant finish.

SERVES 4 PREP: 15 MINUTES COOK: 2 HOURS

1 lb 5 oz salmon steaks, skinned and cut into ¾-1¼-inch pieces

3½ tbsp red curry paste

1⅔ cups/14 fl oz full fat coconut milk

1¼ tbsp fish sauce

1¼ tbsp brown sugar

1⅓ cups green beans, topped with the tails left on

1 green chili, halved lengthwise

1½-inch piece of fresh ginger, finely grated

⅔ cup frozen peas

juice of 1 lime

3½ tbsp chopped fresh cilantro, to garnish

4⅔ cups freshly cooked black rice, to serve

1. Place the salmon, red curry paste, coconut milk, fish sauce, sugar, green beans, chili, and ginger in the slow cooker.

2. Cover the slow cooker, and cook on high for 1 hour 30 minutes. Add the peas, and cook for an additional 20–30 minutes, until the peas are tender. Taste the curry, and add a touch more fish sauce, if liked.

3. Squeeze the lime juice over the curry, and garnish with cilantro. Serve immediately with black rice.

Per serving: 766 cals | 45.7g fat | 24.7g sat fat | 54.4g carbs | 10.3g sugar | 6.2g fiber | 41.1g protein | 1.6g salt

TURKEY CHILI WITH SWEET POTATOES

Add a can of black beans along with the sweet potatoes to feed more people and make this healthy chili even more nutritious.

SERVES 4 PREP: 20 MINUTES COOK: 4 HOURS 10 MINUTES – 8 HOURS 10 MINUTES

1¼ tbsp vegetable oil

1 onion, diced

1½ lb fresh ground turkey

⅓ cup tomato puree

1¼ tbsp mild chili powder

1¼ tsp ground cumin

2 canned chipotle chilies in adobo sauce, de-seeded and diced, plus 2 teaspoons of the adobo sauce (or substitute 1¼ tsp ground chipotles)

1¼ tsp salt

1 x 14 oz can chopped tomatoes

2 cups/16 fl oz chicken stock

1 large sweet potato (about 8 oz), diced

To Serve

1¼ tbsp chopped fresh cilantro

4¾ tbsp sour cream

1 cup/1½ oz grated cheddar cheese

diced avocado

finely chopped red onion

1. Heat the oil in a large frying pan. Add the onion, and cook, stirring, for about 5 minutes, until soft. Add the turkey, and cook, breaking up the meat with a wooden spoon, for about 4 minutes, until brown. Stir in the tomato puree, chili powder, cumin, chilies and adobo sauce, and salt, and cook for an additional 1 minute.

2. Transfer the mixture to the slow cooker. Stir in the tomatoes, stock, and sweet potato. Cover and cook on high for 4 hours or on low for 8 hours. Serve hot, accompanied by the cilantro, sour cream, cheese, avocado, and red onion.

Top Tip

GROUND TURKEY IS A HEALTHY AND LIGHTER ALTERNATIVE TO GROUND BEEF, LAMB, OR PORK.

Per serving: 517 cals | 29.5g fat | 8.4g sat fat | 28.1g carbs | 10.5g sugar | 7g fiber | 38.8g protein | 3.5g salt

CHICKEN IN RIESLING

This is a perfect dish for entertaining. Put it together, then leave it to cook while you make a dessert for your guests.

SERVES 6 PREP: 20–25 MINUTES COOK: 5 HOURS 35 MINUTES – 6 HOURS 35 MINUTES

- 2½ tbsp plain flour
- 1 chicken, weighing 3½ lb, cut into 8 pieces
- ¼ cup/2 oz unsalted butter
- 1¼ tbsp sunflower oil
- 4 shallots, finely chopped
- 12 button mushrooms, sliced
- 2½ tbsp brandy
- 2⅔ cups/17 fl oz Riesling wine
- 1 cup/8 fl oz heavy whipping cream
- salt and pepper (optional)
- 2 cups cooked green beans, to serve
- 1½ cups peas, to serve

1. Put the flour into a freezer bag, and season to taste, if using salt and pepper. Add the chicken pieces, in batches, hold the top securely, and shake well to coat. Transfer the chicken to a plate.

2. Heat half the butter with the oil in a heavy bottom frying pan. Add the chicken pieces and cook over medium–high heat, turning frequently, for 10 minutes, until golden all over. Using a slotted spoon, transfer them to a plate.

3. Wipe out the pan with paper towels, then return to medium–high heat, and melt the remaining butter. Add the shallots and mushrooms and cook, stirring constantly, for 3 minutes. Return the chicken to the frying pan, and remove it from the heat. Warm the brandy in a small ladle, ignite, and carefully pour it over the chicken, shaking the pan gently until the flames have died down.

4. Return the pan to the heat, and pour in the wine. Bring to a boil over low heat, scraping up any sediment from the base of the pan. Transfer to the slow cooker, cover, and cook on low for 5–6 hours, until the chicken is tender and cooked through.

5. Transfer the chicken to a serving dish and keep warm. Skim off any fat from the surface of the cooking liquid, and pour the liquid into a saucepan. Stir in the cream, and bring just to a boil over low heat, and pour over the chicken. Serve immediately with the green vegetables.

Per serving: 946 cals | 60.1g fat | 29.2g sat fat | 26.7g carbs | 12.4g sugar | 5.4g fiber | 50g protein | 0.3g salt

TURKEY BREAST WITH BACON, LEEKS, AND PRUNES

When you have guests but a whole turkey is too much, this elegant dish with one turkey breast will feed up to eight people.

SERVES 8 PREP: 25 MINUTES COOK: 5 HOURS 20 MINUTES – 9 HOURS 20 MINUTES, PLUS RESTING

4 oz back bacon

2 leeks, trimmed, white and light green parts, thinly sliced

1 skinless, bone-in turkey breast (about 4 lb)

3 tbsp flour

1¼ tbsp olive oil, if needed

12 pitted prunes, halved (quartered, if large)

1¼ tsp crumbled dried thyme or 1¼ tbsp finely chopped fresh thyme

1 cup/8 fl oz chicken stock

salt and pepper (optional)

1. Heat a frying pan over a medium–high heat, then add the bacon, and cook until just crisp. Remove from the pan, drain on paper towels, then chop or crumble into small pieces.

2. Add the leeks to the pan, and cook in the bacon fat over a medium–high heat, stirring frequently, for about 5 minutes, or until soft.

3. Season the turkey with salt and pepper, if using, and dredge with the flour. If needed, add the oil to the pan, then add the turkey, and cook on one side for 4–5 minutes, until brown. Turn, and cook on the other side for an additional 4–5 minutes, until brown.

4. Place the turkey in the slow cooker together with the leeks, bacon, prunes, and thyme. Add the stock, cover, and cook on high for about 5 hours or on low for about 9 hours.

5. Remove the turkey from the slow cooker, and let rest for 5 minutes. Slice, and serve with some of the sauce, including the prunes and bits of bacon spooned over the top.

Top Tip

PRUNES GIVE A LITTLE MORE SWEETNESS TO THIS TURKEY DISH—THEY ALSO OFFER A RICH SUPPLY OF POTASSIUM AND VITAMIN C.

Per serving: 371 cals | 8.6g fat | 2.2g sat fat | 15.7g carbs | 6.4g sugar | 1.6g fiber | 56g protein | 1.3g salt

HONEY-GLAZED DUCK LEGS

This elegant alternative to chicken legs creates an unforgettable dinner party dish with very little preparation.

SERVES 6 PREP: 15 MINUTES COOK: 6 HOURS 20 MINUTES – 10 HOURS 20 MINUTES

6 duck legs

½ cup/4 fl oz chicken stock

3½ tbsp red wine or white wine

⅓ cup clear honey

1¼ tbsp fresh thyme leaves

salt and pepper (optional)

2¼ cups mashed potatoes, to serve

1. Trim any excess skin or fat from the duck legs, and season with salt and pepper, if using. Heat a large heavy bottom frying pan over medium–high heat. When the pan is very hot, add the duck legs, in batches, if necessary, and cook on one side for about 4 minutes, until brown. Turn, and cook on the other side for about 4 minutes, until brown. Transfer to the slow cooker.

2. Put the stock, wine, honey, and thyme into a small bowl, stir to combine, then pour the mixture over the duck legs, turning to coat. Cover, and cook on high for about 6 hours or on low for about 10 hours, until the duck is very tender. Serve hot with mashed potatoes.

Top Tip

YOU CAN DRIZZLE ANY EXCESS HONEY JUICES FROM THE SLOW COOKER OVER THE DUCK LEGS BEFORE SERVING.

Per serving: 362 cals | 11.2g fat | 3.1g sat fat | 36.7g carbs | 17.3g sugar | 1.8g fiber | 26.9g protein | 1.3g salt

SLOW DOWN AND BE WOWED

You've had your slow cooker for a while and it has a regular place in your kitchen. Your family loves the wafting aromas of meaty stocks and flavor-infused vegetables when they come home in the evening and the memorable meals that the slow cooker serves up. You love the convenience and the deep flavors of the soups, casseroles, and pot roasts that have become part of your daily routine. So now it's time to raise your game, invite some guests over and impress them with your slow cooker regime.

SPEND TIME WITH YOUR GUESTS

When it comes to wow factor, there is often some preparation involved. However, the advantage of a slow cooker, even when preparing more ambitious recipes, is that many recipes don't have elaborate processes once the slow cooker has done its job. Think of Beef Ribs Braised in Red Wine—once they are in the slow cooker they just need serving up, perhaps with the addition of mashed potatoes, rice, or polenta. This means you've still got plenty of time to spend chatting with your guests.

AWESOME DISHES

If you like to keep it simple, producing an amazing slow cooker meal doesn't have to eat up your precious time. Clams in Spicy Broth with Chorizo, for example, is a delicious offering for a light meal where the slow cooker does all the hard work—the clams are added for the final 15 minutes and, served with crusty bread, the clam-filled spectacle will be a surefire hit.

If your choice of dish needs a big wow factor, try Butternut Squash and Goat cheese Enchiladas. Once the roasted squash is prepared, the sauce with onions, tomatoes, and honey is layered in the slow cooker with the tortillas, squash, and cheese. Two hours later you have your meal. Another option is Mini Chicken Potpies—the potpie mixture is prepared in the slow cooker, added to ramekins, topped with pastry, and browned for 20 minutes (still leaving plenty of time for socializing).

SWEET AND SLOW

When it comes to desserts, the slow cooker offers a surprising number of options. Crème brûlée is the sort of sweet, smooth dish that you might always zoom in on when dining out but never think of making at home. But all you have to do is get out your slow cooker!

And who would think you could make a strawberry cheesecake in a slow cooker? Well, you can—add the biscuit base and the fruity cheesecake mixture to a springform pan, put it in the slow cooker, and leave it for two hours—afterward letting it cool and then decorating with strawberries. Guaranteed to be a mealtime talking point!

BUTTERNUT SQUASH AND GOAT CHEESE ENCHILADAS

Roasting butternut squash caramelizes it, giving an enticing sweetness that balances out the spicy sauce and salty cheese.

SERVES 4 PREP: 35–40 MINUTES COOK: 2 HOURS 50 MINUTES – 3 HOURS

1 large butternut squash, peeled and diced

4¾ tbsp olive oil

1¼ tsp salt

3 tsp ground cumin

1 large onion, diced

3 garlic cloves, finely chopped

1¼ tbsp hot or mild chili powder

1¼ tbsp dried oregano

1 lb canned chopped tomatoes or tomato passata

1¼ tbsp clear honey

1½ cups/16 fl oz vegetable stock

12 corn tortillas

225 g/8 oz soft, fresh goat cheese

1. Preheat the oven to 400°F. Line a baking sheet with parchment paper. Coat the squash with 2 tablespoons of the oil, sprinkle with half the salt and 1 teaspoon of the cumin. Place the squash on the baking sheet, and roast for 30–40 minutes, until soft and beginning to brown.

2. Heat the remaining oil in a large frying pan over medium–high heat. Add the onion and garlic, and cook, stirring, for about 5 minutes, until soft. Add the remaining cumin and salt, the chili powder, and the oregano, and cook for an additional 1 minute. Stir in the tomatoes, honey, and stock, bring to a boil, and cook for about 5 minutes. Purée the sauce in a food processor or blender.

3. Coat the base of the slow cooker with a little sauce. Make a layer of tortillas, tearing them if necessary, to cover the bottom of the slow cooker. Top the tortillas with a layer of the squash, a layer of cheese, a layer of sauce, then another layer of tortillas.

4. Layer again with squash, cheese, and sauce. Finish with a layer of tortillas, sauce, and the remaining cheese. Cover and cook on low for 2 hours, until the tortillas are soft and the cheese is melted and bubbling. Serve hot.

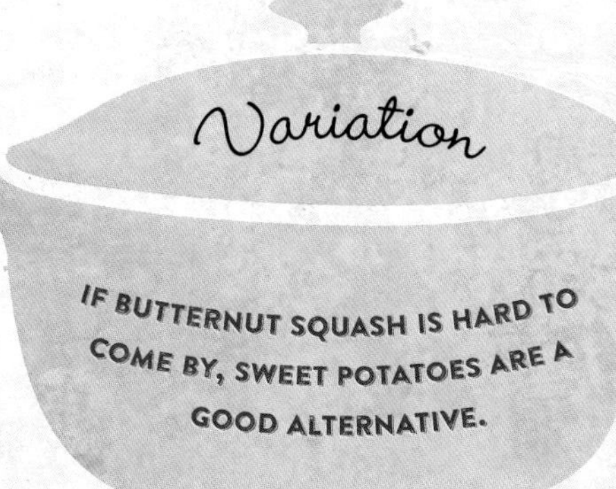

Per serving: 362 cals | 11.2g fat | 3.1g sat fat | 36.7g carbs | 17.3g sugar | 1.8g fiber | 26.9g protein | 1.3g salt

BEEF RIBS BRAISED IN RED WINE

This dish is incredibly tender and packed with flavor—serve with mashed potatoes or polenta to make the most of the rich sauce.

SERVES 6 PREP: 20 MINUTES COOK: 7 HOURS 40 MINUTES – 10 HOURS 40 MINUTES

3 lb bone-in beef short ribs

2½ tbsp vegetable oil, plus extra, if needed

1 onion, diced

1 celery stick, diced

1 carrot, diced

1¼ tbsp tomato puree

3 fresh thyme sprigs

2 garlic cloves, finely chopped

3½ tbsp plain flour

2 cups/16 fl oz red wine

1 cup/8 fl oz beef stock

1 bay leaf

salt and pepper (optional)

2¼ cups mashed potatoes, to serve

1. Generously season the ribs with salt and pepper, if using. Heat the oil in a large, heavy bottom frying pan over medium–high heat. Add the ribs, and cook, turning occasionally, for about 10 minutes, until brown on all sides. Transfer to the slow cooker.

2. Add more oil to the pan if needed, and, when hot, add the onion, celery, and carrot to the pan. Cook, stirring occasionally, for about 15 minutes, until the vegetables are soft. Add the tomato puree, thyme, garlic, and flour, and cook, stirring, for an additional 1 minute.

3. Add the wine, bring to a boil, and cook for an additional 1–2 minutes, stirring and scraping up any sediment from the base of the pan. Reduce heat to medium–low, and simmer for 6–8 minutes, until the liquid is reduced by about half. Transfer to the slow cooker.

4. Stir in the stock, ½ teaspoon of salt, and the bay leaf, cover, and cook on high for 7 hours or on low for 10 hours, until the meat is very tender and falling from the bone. About 1–2 hours before the end of cooking, set the lid ajar, if desired, to allow the liquid to reduce and reach a thicker consistency.

5. Before serving, remove and discard the thyme and bay leaf. Serve hot with the mashed potatoes.

Per serving: 504 cals | 22.1g fat | 8g sat fat | 29.5g carbs | 4g sugar | 2.7g fiber | 31g protein | 1.7g salt

MINI CHICKEN POTPIES

There's no better treat than a freshly made mini chicken potpie, and you don't have to spend hours over a hot stove for this version!

SERVES 6 PREP: 30 MINUTES, PLUS COOLING COOK: 4 HOURS 40 MINUTES – 8 HOURS 40 MINUTES

- 3½ tbsp butter
- 1 onion, diced
- ½ cup button mushrooms, diced
- 1½ lb boneless, skinless chicken, diced
- 1 carrot, diced
- 2 celery sticks, diced
- 1¼ tbsp fresh thyme leaves
- 2½ tbsp plain flour, plus 2 tsp, for dusting
- 1 cup/8 fl oz milk
- ¾ cup/6 fl oz chicken stock
- 1¼ tsp salt
- ½ tsp pepper
- 2 sheets ready-rolled puff pastry

1. Melt 1 tablespoon of the butter in a large frying pan over medium–high heat. Add the onion, and cook, stirring, for about 5 minutes, until soft. Add the mushrooms, and cook, stirring, for an additional 3 minutes, or until the mushrooms are beginning to soften. Transfer the mixture to the slow cooker, and add the chicken, carrot, celery, and thyme.

2. Reduce the heat under the frying pan to medium, add the remaining butter, and heat until melted. Whisk in the flour, and cook, whisking constantly, until the mixture is lightly browned and begins to give off a nutty aroma. Whisk in the milk, stock, salt, and pepper, and continue to cook, stirring, for an additional 5 minutes, or until the mixture begins to thicken.

3. Add the mixture to the slow cooker and stir to mix well. Cover, and cook on high for about 4 hours or on low for about 8 hours, until the chicken is tender and the sauce has thickened. Divide the filling equally between 6 x 8 fl oz ramekins.

4. Preheat the oven to 375°F. Roll out the pastry on a lightly floured surface and cut out six rounds, each about 1 inch larger in circumference than the ramekins. Top each filled ramekin with a pastry round, crimping the edges. Prick the pastry on each pie several times with a fork.

5. Place the ramekins on a baking sheet and bake in the preheated oven for about 20 minutes, until the pastry is puffed and golden brown. Let cool for about 10 minutes before serving.

Per serving: 593 cals | 34.4g fat | 16.4g sat fat | 38.6g carbs | 5g sugar | 2.9g fiber | 30.6g protein | 2.2g salt

CLAMS IN SPICY BROTH WITH CHORIZO

This festive, yet simple shellfish dish makes a lovely light meal served with a crisp green salad and fresh crusty bread to soak up the delicious broth.

SERVES 8 PREP: 25 MINUTES COOK: 2 HOURS 25 MINUTES – 4 HOURS 25 MINUTES

1¼ tbsp olive oil

1 red onion, halved lengthwise and sliced

4 oz chorizo sausage, diced

1 fennel bulb, coarsely chopped

1 x 14 oz can chopped tomatoes, with juice

½ cup/4 fl oz dry white wine

½ cup/4 fl oz clam juice or water

½ tsp salt

¼–½ tsp crushed red pepper flakes

2 lb small clams, scrubbed

2½ tbsp chopped fresh flat-leaf parsley, to garnish

2 cups green salad, to serve

crusty bread (about 6 oz), to serve

1. Heat the oil in a large frying pan over medium–high heat. Add the onion, and cook, stirring, for about 5 minutes, until soft. Add the chorizo, and continue to cook, stirring occasionally, until the meat begins to brown. Transfer the mixture to the slow cooker.

2. Stir in the fennel, tomatoes and their can juices, wine, clam juice, salt, and red pepper flakes. Cover, and cook on high for about 2 hours or on low for about 4 hours.

3. Discard any clams with broken shells and any that refuse to close when tapped. Add the clams to the slow cooker, cover, and cook on high for an additional 10–15 minutes, until the clams have opened. Discard any clams that remain closed.

4. Serve the clams in bowls, with a generous amount of broth, garnished with parsley, and accompanied by the green salad and crusty bread.

Per serving: 782 cals | 33.9g fat | 10.2g sat fat | 71.6g carbs | 15.6g sugar | 8.6g fiber | 36.9g protein | 5.8g salt

WILD MUSHROOM LASAGNA

You can use your slow cooker like a lasagna dish, layering up the ingredients and then leaving the slow cooker to its own devices.

SERVES 6 PREP: 35 MINUTES, PLUS SOAKING COOK: 4 HOURS 35 MINUTES

1¼ tbsp vegetable oil, for brushing

8 lasagna noodles

2 tbsp/1 oz freshly grated Parmesan cheese

Filling

2½ tbsp dried porcini mushrooms

2 cups/16 fl oz boiling water

2½ tbsp olive oil

1 small onion, diced

2 garlic cloves, finely chopped

5 cups button mushrooms or chestnut mushrooms, sliced

½ cup/4 fl oz red wine

1¼ tbsp finely chopped fresh thyme leaves

½ tsp salt

½ tsp pepper

Sauce

¼ cup/2 oz unsalted butter

⅓ cup plain flour

2½ cups/19¼ fl oz milk

⅔ cup/3 oz freshly grated Parmesan cheese

¾ tsp salt

1. To make the filling, soak the porcini mushrooms in the water for 30 minutes. Remove the mushrooms, reserving the liquid, and chop. Heat the oil in a large frying pan over medium–high heat. Add the onion and garlic, and cook, stirring, for 5 minutes. Add the fresh and reconstituted mushrooms, and cook, stirring, for about 5 minutes, until soft. Add the wine, bring to a boil, and cook for about 5 minutes, until the liquid has almost evaporated. Add the mushroom-soaking liquid, thyme, salt, and pepper, and cook over medium–high heat, stirring frequently, for an additional 5 minutes, or until the liquid is reduced by half.

2. To make the sauce, melt the butter in a large saucepan over medium heat. Whisk in the flour, and cook, whisking constantly, for about 3 minutes, until the mixture is golden brown. Whisk in the milk, and bring to a boil. Reduce the heat, and simmer for 3 minutes, then remove from the heat, and stir in the cheese and salt.

3. To assemble the lasagna, line the slow cooker with foil, overlapping two large pieces to cover the entire base. Lightly brush the foil with oil. Spoon a thin layer of sauce and a thin layer of filling over the base. Top with a layer of pasta. Repeat twice, finishing with a final layer of pasta and then a layer of sauce. Top with a final layer of pasta, then a layer of sauce. Sprinkle the cheese over the top. Cover, and cook on low for about 4 hours, until the pasta is tender and the top is brown and bubbling. Serve the lasagna directly from the slow cooker or use the foil as a sling to lift it out to serve.

Per serving: 476 cals | 23.8g fat | 10.8g sat fat | 45.3g carbs | 8.1g sugar | 2.9g fiber | 18.1g protein | 2g salt

CRÈME BRÛLÉE

Everyone loves a crème brûlée, but not everyone has it as a regular dinner party pleaser—just sit back and enjoy the glory.

MAKES 6 PREP: 20 MINUTES, PLUS INFUSING, COOLING, AND CHILLING COOK: 3 HOURS 5 MINUTES – 3 HOURS 35 MINUTES

1 vanilla bean

4 cups/32 fl oz heavy whipping cream

6 egg yolks

½ cup superfine sugar

⅓ cup light brown sugar

1. Using a sharp knife, split the vanilla bean in half lengthwise, scrape the seeds into a saucepan, and add the pod. Pour in the cream and bring just to a boil, stirring constantly. Remove from heat, cover, and leave to infuse for 20 minutes.

2. Whisk together the egg yolks and superfine sugar in a bowl until thoroughly mixed. Remove and discard the vanilla bean from the pan, then whisk the cream into the egg yolk mixture. Strain the mixture into a large pitcher.

3. Divide the mixture between 6 x 4 fl oz ramekins, and cover with foil. Stand the ramekins on a trivet in the slow cooker and pour in enough boiling water to come about halfway up the sides of the ramekins. Cover and cook on low for 3–3½ hours, until just set. Remove the slow cooker insert from the base, and let cool completely, then remove the ramekins, and chill in the refrigerator for at least 4 hours.

4. Preheat the broiler. Sprinkle the brown sugar evenly over the surface of each dessert, then cook under the broiler for 30–60 seconds, until the sugar has melted and caramelized. Alternatively, you can use a cook's blowtorch. Return the ramekins to the refrigerator, and chill for an additional hour before serving.

Per serving: 474 cals | 16.7g fat | 4.5g sat fat | 82.8g carbs | 59.3g sugar | 5.7g fiber | 4.3g protein | 0.2g salt

STRAWBERRY CHEESECAKE

This excellent cheesecake has a creamy strawberry filling—and who would have thought you could make this in a slow cooker?

SERVES 8 PREP: 20 MINUTES, PLUS COOLING COOK: 2 HOURS 5 MINUTES, PLUS STANDING

- 1/3 cup/3 oz unsalted butter, melted
- 1 1/2 cup graham crackers, crushed
- 2 cups strawberries, hulled
- 1 lb 5 oz cream cheese
- 1 cup superfine sugar
- 2 large eggs, beaten
- 2 1/2 tbsp cornstarch
- finely grated rind and juice of 1 lemon

1. Stir the butter into the crushed graham crackers, and press into the base of a 8-inch round springform pan, or a pan that fits into your slow cooker.

2. Purée or mash half the strawberries, and whisk together with the cheese, sugar, eggs, cornstarch, and lemon rind and juice until smooth.

3. Tip the mixture into the pan and place in the slow cooker. Cover and cook on high for about 2 hours or until almost set.

4. Turn off the slow cooker and leave the cheesecake in the cooker for 2 hours. Remove and cool completely, then carefully turn out of the pan.

5. Decorate with the remaining sliced strawberries and serve.

Variation

YOU COULD REPLACE THE STRAWBERRIES WITH RASPBERRIES OR OTHER BERRIES IF YOU PREFER.

Per serving: 491 cals | 30.1g fat | 18.6g sat fat | 47.8g carbs | 36.1g sugar | 1.6g fiber | 7.7g protein | 0.8g salt

BUTTERSCOTCH PUDDING

This rich and creamy butterscotch pudding is divinely easy to make in the slow cooker.

MAKES 6 PREP: 20 MINUTES, PLUS COOLING AND CHILLING COOK: 2 HOURS 5 MINUTES

2½ tbsp unsalted butter

1⅓ cups dark brown sugar

½ tsp salt

1¼ cup/10 fl oz heavy whipping cream

¾ cup/6 fl oz milk

4 egg yolks, lightly beaten

2½ tsp vanilla extract

2½ tsp whisky

2 tbsp/1 fl oz heavy whipping cream, whipped, to serve

1. Fill the slow cooker with water to a depth of about 1½ inches.

2. Melt the butter in a large saucepan over medium heat. Add the sugar and salt, and stir to mix well. Add the cream and milk, and heat over a medium heat, until hot but not boiling.

3. Place the egg yolks in a medium-sized mixing bowl. Add the sugar and milk mixture in a very thin stream, whisking constantly. Whisk in the vanilla extract and whisky. Ladle the mixture into 6 x 4 fl oz ramekins.

4. Carefully place the ramekins in the slow cooker, taking care not to slosh any of the water into them. Cover the slow cooker and cook on low for about 2 hours, or until the puddings are set.

5. Remove the ramekins from the slow cooker and transfer to a wire rack to cool for about 15 minutes, then cover with plastic wrap, place in the refrigerator, and chill for at least 2 hours before serving. Serve chilled, topped with a dollop of whipped cream.

Variation

VANILLA ICE CREAM IS ANOTHER WINNING SERVING SUGGESTION.

Per serving: 521 cals | 33.9g fat | 20.4g sat fat | 48.5g carbs | 48g sugar | 0g fiber | 3.6g protein | 0.5g salt

INDEX